LIVING LEAVEN FREE

CLEAN

LIVING LEAVEN FREE

ROD PARSLEY

Clean: Living Leaven Free

ISBN: 978-0-578-47950-7

Copyright © 2019 by Rod Parsley

Published by:

Results Publishing

P.O. Box 100

Columbus, Ohio 43216-0100 USA

Unless otherwise indicated, all Scripture quotations are taken from the Modern English Version of the Bible. Copyright © 2014 by Military Bible Association. Used by permission. All rights reserved.

Printed in the United States of America. All rights reserved under International Copyright Law. Contents and/or cover may not be reproduced in whole or in part in any form without the expressed written consent of the Publisher.

DEDICATION

I am grateful for my parents who trained me in the things of God.

In the early days of World Harvest Church, they enabled me to concentrate on my studies in Bible college, on building the church, and on deepening my walk with the Lord. They stood by me then, and their memory inspires me today.

In my life, I have known no greater man than my father. Some of the most powerful experiences I remember are from my childhood when my father would gather us in the living room. I can still hear him pray: "God, this is my family. And God, we need you. We need you in our family. We're not going to let the devil have our family." His undying hope in God was the anchor of his soul.

My mother's lifestyle set a standard that has stayed with me to this day. From her I learned respect for the Word of God. She taught me by example to approach God's throne of grace with confidence. She was a praying mother whose passion and determination became patterns for my life.

When I was eight years old, I heard her praying and weeping in her prayer closet: *"God, please save my children."*

And He did! Because He saved me and subsequently called me to the ministry, He has surely impacted untold, multiplied thousands of lives as a result of the work He has called me to do in four decades of public Gospel ministry.

I lovingly dedicate this book to the memory of my parents, James and Ellen Parsley. I miss them every day, but I know where they are and I look forward to being reunited with them in heaven one day!

Luke 16:11 was fulfilled in my parents: *So if you have not been faithful in the unrighteous wealth, who will commit to your trust the true riches?*

I thank you, Dad and Mom, for the Biblical teaching you faithfully instilled in me from an early age and for the godly example you entrusted in me.

TABLE OF CONTENTS

PROLOGUE   1
One Small Drop

INTRODUCTION   5
How Spiritual Deterioration Contaminates the Unsuspecting Church

CHAPTER 1   23
The Corrosive Effects of Leaven

CHAPTER 2   41
Leaven of the Pharisees

CHAPTER 3   73
The Leaven of the Sadducees

CHAPTER 4   107
The Leaven of the Herodians

CHAPTER 5   127
The Leaven of the Corinthians

CHAPTER 6   147
The Leaven of the Galatians

CHAPTER 7   179
The Cleansing Solution

PROLOGUE
ONE SMALL DROP

A drop of water fell onto an iron support beam of a beautiful old bridge. Slowly, steadily, the drops continued to fall, endlessly tapping the beam.

Slowly, a corrosive chemical reaction began within the metal. The bridge gleamed beautifully for all to see, but none noticed the decay growing inside of it. The drops continued, feeding the deterioration. A light shell of rust began to form, adding color and texture to the appearance of the beautiful old bridge. Months passed, and the contamination spread.

One day, the townsfolk decided to restore the graceful old bridge to its original beauty. As the workers prepared the bridge for a fresh coat of paint, they discovered the corrosion in time to cut it out.

If the rust had not been noticed and dealt with quickly, disaster would have struck. If it had been ignored, and allowed to work its way through the iron beam, the damage that initially only penetrated the surface would have gone to the very core of the beam.

The strength of the metal would have been weakened beyond repair. Ultimately, the bridge would have fallen with a crash, taking unsuspecting travelers with it into the dark chasm below.

God uses similar imagery in the Bible to warn us about the damaging effects of sin in our lives. A loaf of bread rises because yeast has fermented inside the dough, causing air bubbles to lighten the texture of the dough. Although leavening is good for bread, in the Bible it is frequently used as a metaphor for sin. Like a pinch of yeast leavening its way through a lump of dough, sin can permeate every fiber of our being. But praise God, it doesn't have to be that way!

When we are careful to live in the loving and obedient ways of God, and when we do not allow the corrosive elements of life to infect our walk with Him, He can—and will—reward us, because He loves to abundantly bless His people.

My prayer for you is that you will be richly blessed as you discover in these pages how you can walk in God's mighty power and glory!

INTRODUCTION
HOW SPIRITUAL DETERIORATION CONTAMINATES THE UNSUSPECTING CHURCH

I can still remember what it felt like, a quarter of a century later.

What a sense of delight and anticipation I felt as I held the first copy of *Repairers of the Breach* in my hands. For an entire year, I lived with that God-given message–preaching it, rejoicing in it, drawing it deep into my spirit. Then, He commissioned me to commit His message to print.

On that day in 1992, I was overjoyed with what I felt was the completion of the task the Lord had set before me, and I rejoiced in anticipation of how many lives God would change through the spiritual truths contained in the book.

But God cut my celebration short. "You're not finished yet," He told me in the midst of my elation.

"What? What do you mean, Lord?" I asked, puzzled and surprised.

"You've only delivered the first half of My message," He replied.

Repairers of the Breach was birthed from Isaiah 58:12:

> *Those from among you shall rebuild the old waste places; you shall raise up the foundations of many generations; and you shall be called, the Repairer of the Breach, the Restorer of Paths in which to Dwell.*

In the Garden of Eden, man committed sin. That sin opened a breach—a chasm between God and man, into which man fell. As a result, suffering, crying humanity desperately needed a way to bridge that chasm and to experience the life-giving hope and joy of God.

From the moment man fell, God began building a bridge to repair the breach, so man could return to a place of fellowship with Him. The bridge God built across that chasm was the Cross, and on it He put His only Son. He shed the sinless blood of a crucified carpenter from

INTRODUCTION

Nazareth on a bridge Satan could never cross:

> *But he was wounded for our transgressions, he was bruised for our iniquities; the chastisement of our peace was upon him, and by his stripes we are healed* (Isaiah 53:5).

The chasm between God and man was spanned through the suffering of Jesus. He bridged the gap between sin-infected man and a holy God, and He gave us access to a life of victory. No longer must we be subject to the tactics of the enemy. Jesus reached across the Gospel bridge. He pushed back the forces of darkness, and He gave us the foundational planks of power to keep His bridge strong. God's spotless Lamb delivered us from the shackles and chains of bondage and gave us the freedom to choose to live holy and victorious lives!

We Can Restore the Battered Planks of the Gospel Bridge!

In *Repairers of the Breach* I shared seven

foundational truths, vital planks in the Gospel bridge that had been taken by the devil. One by one, we restored the planks that Satan had ripped up. God showed me how to secure each of those planks onto the Gospel bridge —a bridge mankind can only cross through the blood of Jesus.

Today, Jesus sits at the right hand of the Father to bring us across the bridge, from where we are to where we can be.

- From sorrow to success.
- From poverty to prosperity.
- From the gutter to glory.
- From victim to victory.
- From hell to heaven!

I was eager to understand the second half of the message God wanted me to deliver. So, I asked, "Lord I have painstakingly exposed what Satan has stolen from the Church. What would you have me do now?"

"Read the verse again," He answered. So I did:

Those from among you shall rebuild the old waste places; you shall raise up the foundations of many generations; and you shall be called, the Repairer of the Breach, the Restorer of Paths in which to Dwell (Isaiah 58:12).

I saw that God wants His Church to move beyond repairing the breach to restoring the paths in which it should dwell.

Then God began to reveal to me the truths contained in this book.

Repairers of the Breach awakened the Church to what has been stolen from us by the devil and showed the body of Christ how to repair the loss. But "repair" is different from "restore."

Yes, the troops have been mustered. We have strapped on the armor of God. Our feet are shod with the preparation of the Gospel of peace. We've girded our loins with truth, put on the breastplate of righteousness, donned the helmet of salvation, armed ourselves with the shield of faith and the sword of the Spirit. The bridge has been repaired. But Satan has been subtly chipping away at the newly installed Gospel planks on that bridge, until once again they are becoming weak and brittle, making the crossing precarious and unsure.

We can repair a compromised bridge. But if we don't carefully watch and protect that beam, corrosion can—like a pinch of leaven—weaken the beam until, one day, it will fall with a great crash. The process is slow, almost imperceptible. But it proceeds patiently, doing its work until it spreads throughout crucial areas, saps the strength of the beam, and brings about collapse and ruin.

God showed me that the Church not only needs to repair the gaps in the Gospel bridge with strong Gospel planks, but it also needs to restore the bridge to its full strength and eliminate the leaven that caused the breach. We must learn how to recognize the subtle, corrosive attacks of the devil as he attempts to weaken the bridge.

I have great hope that the Church will assume its God-given position of authority over the powers of darkness and rebuke Satan from continuing to weaken the Gospel bridge from beneath our feet! And through the grace of God, there is a Way to do just that!

INTRODUCTION

SUBTLE SEDUCTION, DEADLY DECEPTION

Movies and television programs around the world portray sex outside a marriage relationship as fun, exciting and seductive. It is presented as a spontaneous experience, with no negative repercussions, something that everyone is encouraged and entitled to engage in. Too often, the message of these programs is, "Sex is a wonderful adventure. Do it, whether you are married or not, whether you know the person or not, whether you are the same sex or not. Just do it, and make it spontaneous! Fun! Wild! Kinky!"

Uh-huh. By now almost everyone knows that sex outside of God's design for marriage has all kinds of negative repercussions.

I grow weary of attending funerals for cancer victims, only to hear somebody declare to me, "It must have been God's will to pick another flower for the garden of heaven." How subtle are the devil's deceptions!

But is it possible that these diseases could be mere forerunners of an even deadlier disease yet to hit the world? More importantly, is there any way to prevent

that ghastly possibility from coming to pass?
Yes, thank God, there is.

SPIRITUAL DISEASE IN THE CHURCH

Just as diseases are eating away the physical fiber of a generation, the moral fabric of the Church today is in danger of being destroyed by an even deadlier spiritual parasite.

> *My son, attend to my words; incline your ear to my sayings. Do not let them depart from your eyes; keep them in the midst of your heart; for they are life to those who find them, and health to all their body. Keep your heart with all diligence, for out of it are the issues of life.*
>
> (Proverbs 4:20-23)

In the above passage, the word "keep" means "to guard." God is telling us to guard our heart with diligence, to keep it as pure as a loving father would his own virgin daughter.

INTRODUCTION

God wants the Church to know that the Gospel planks have been put back into place on the Gospel bridge, and now we must guard them from the eroding lies and deceptions of the enemy.

It is time to tell Satan to take his hands off our families and get out of our lives. It is time to root out and remove the leaven of Lucifer. It is time to proclaim to the devil, "This old Gospel bridge does not belong to you! We are fed up with you slipping in and corroding the strength of the body of Christ! Enough!"

Satan has two predominant tactics in eroding the planks of the Gospel. First, he steals. Jesus said, "The thief does not come, except to steal and kill and destroy. I came that they may have life, and that they may have it more abundantly" (John 10:10).

A thief does not have to be strong to steal. All he needs to do is enter your home when you are gone, when your house is left unprotected, and you are unaware.

The devil can enter our lives without force when we knowingly continue in sin, when we fail to pray, when we straddle the fence between sanctification and sin, when we are not walking in the fullness of the power of God and filled with His Spirit. This is happening in many churches.

"The services look good," we say, satisfied with ourselves. "The sound system works great. There was a good turnout at the last church event. We're on the right road." But too often, our churches are not on the road God would have them travel.

While we congratulate ourselves on our marvelous music ministry or evangelism program, do we realize that nearly one-third of Christians believe adultery between consenting, married adults is acceptable? When we rejoice in the dedicated and select few who attend Bible studies, do we know that almost two-thirds of self-professed Christians in America cannot name the four Gospels?

Are we vigilant in Biblical doctrines and truths, or have we left ourselves spiritually unprotected? Are we in danger of becoming complacent and apathetic about spiritual viruses that are ravaging our beloved Church? Or has the disease spread so subtly that we don't even see the danger—to the point where soon we may be unable to protect ourselves against its damaging conclusion?

There are ways the Church can be more zealous in guarding the doctrines Christ put in place so we can lead productive, joyful, victorious lives. We can resist the insidious leaven of spiritual disease and prevent it from spreading throughout the entire Church. All we need to do is stand firm against humanistic theologians who would eliminate from our services soul-saving songs about the saving, purifying, sanctifying blood of our Lord Jesus Christ. We need to show the door to those who would avoid preaching life-changing sermons about the Second Coming of Christ and begin teaching unashamedly about the doctrines of sin and of eternal judgment.

If we will abide in hope, reverse the trend, repair the breach and restore the bridge, we will have complete victory over the devil in every way. And the last laugh will belong to God, for He is in command and He has a plan in place to reverse this leaven and end its deadly effects!

As the apostle Paul wrote, "And hope does not disappoint, because the love of God is shed abroad in our hearts by the Holy Spirit who has been given to us" (Romans 5:5).

THERE IS HOPE!

In *Repairers of the Breach* I shared how we can restore the paths God would have us dwell in. I explained how to repair the planks the devil had ripped from the Gospel bridge.

God has shown me that many of the planks we have put back into our Gospel bridge appear stable, but are cracked and rotting underneath. There is a spiritual disease within that is worse than the world's physical diseases, and it is eating away at the body of Christ.

Satan has employed a deadly scheme of destroying, undermining and diluting the basic truths of the Gospel by sowing leaven into the unleavened bread of the children of God. It is time to expose this devastating scheme of the devil; and once exposed, to take out the weakened planks and replace them with pure, unadulterated, foundational truths, to be kept solid and unblemished until Jesus returns.

In Galatians 5:9, Paul says, "A little yeast leavens the whole batch." Leaven is spiritual disease. It has no odor. You cannot see it. You cannot detect it with the senses. Leaven works secretly and silently. It does not walk up and say, "Hello, I am error in the Church, and I am here to lead you on a path of destruction and damn your soul to hell. Follow me." Instead, leaven hides itself within the trappings of religion.

Satan does not have any new tricks. He is using the same tactics he has always used to dilute and destroy the truths of the Gospel. And his tactics have been published: they're in Scripture! The Bible gives us information about five forms of deadly leaven:

1. The Leaven of the Pharisees

2. The Leaven of the Sadducees

3. The Leaven of the Herodians

4. The Leaven of the Corinthians

5. The Leaven of the Galatians

In this book I am going to show you how to discern, expose, and eradicate each of these types of leaven.

God says all leaven must be removed:

Seven days shall there be no leaven found in your houses, for whoever eats that which is leavened, that person shall be cut off from the congregation of Israel, whether he be a stranger or born in the land. You shall eat nothing leavened. In all your dwellings you shall eat unleavened bread (Exodus 12:19-20).

THE ROAD TO DEATH

In 1989, the night before the notorious serial killer Ted Bundy was executed, I watched as Dr. James Dobson interviewed him on television. Bundy demonically murdered, raped, and ravaged many women. Yet, according to various newspaper accounts, he was raised in a Christian home!

As he sat handcuffed in his jail cell, Bundy told Dr. Dobson that he shuddered to think of the kind of people who were walking loose in our society at the time because our society had become so infested with pornography. He confessed to Dr. Dobson how his road to sin started: "I found a few discarded magazines along the roadway. As a young boy, I began to feed myself on the images in those magazines, to fuel my thoughts, until they suddenly grasped hold of me and would not let go."

Now remember, Bundy was talking about an era when pornography was harder to find. X-rated movies weren't available on pay-per-view television, 'skin' magazines couldn't be found at the corner convenience store, and a man couldn't invite it into his family's home via the Internet while his unsuspecting wife and children slept in adjacent rooms. A form of leaven was brought into young Ted Bundy's home, and eventually his entire moral structure collapsed from the corrosive nature of the sin of pornography.

With the dramatic increase of access to pornography today via the Internet, television, and the neighborhood store, you can only imagine the ticking human time bombs being created by the vile leaven of pornography.

Each particle of leaven pollutes the body of Christ like a land mine. It remains hidden just below the surface until it is suddenly triggered into a spiritual explosion, ultimately blasting its victim with such destruction and devastation that there is nothing left but death.

BEWARE THE GENERALIZED GOSPEL

Jesus said,

In vain do they worship Me, teaching as doctrines the precepts of men. For laying aside the commandment of God, you hold the tradition of men—the washing of pitchers and cups, and many other such things you do (Mark 7:7-8).

The generalized Gospel is one that preaches an all-inclusive, non-condemning, watered-down version of Christianity. Its goal is not salvation, but pacification.

It is time to return to the narrow path. We are the living remnant of the Church of Jesus Christ of Nazareth

INTRODUCTION

—washed in the blood, bought with a price, redeemed from every nation, filled with the Holy Ghost, looking for the Second Coming, and operating in signs, wonders, and apostolic authority!

Isn't it time we resist the traditions of men? Isn't it time to shout out that even a little bit of compromise plays into the hands of the adversary? Our planks have been weakened! Satan has sown leaven into unleavened truth and mixed tares in with wheat! We know what the fate will be of both those who hold fast to the true Gospel and those who are seduced by a generalized Gospel. Jesus said,

> *Let both grow together until the harvest, and in the time of harvest I will say to the reapers: Gather up the weeds first and bind them in bundles to burn them, but gather the wheat into my barn* (Matthew 13:30).

Are you as fed up as I am of Christians remaining silent while organized prayer remains banned from our schools and from our heritage? Are you as disgusted as I am with church denominations that ordain and celebrate openly homosexual ministers? Are you as appalled as I am about the evil leaven that is seeping into the Church? Then it's time to return to the blood-bought Gospel of Jesus Christ!

Come with me and let us search out and destroy the rotten planks of religious traditionalism and blasphemy, and restore the Gospel bridge with sturdy, incorruptible planks. We know what leaven does: "A little bit of leaven ruins the whole lump." Just a little bit! The faith of a mustard seed can move a mighty mountain, yet a little leaven will ruin your whole heart, your whole mind, your whole will.

Is there hope? Yes! And He's in you: "To them God would make known what is the glorious riches of this mystery among the nations. It is Christ in you, the hope of glory" (Colossians 1:27).

Continue with me in the pages that follow and discover how we can get the leaven out of our lives and walk in the power and glory of God.

CHAPTER 1

THE CORROSIVE EFFECTS OF LEAVEN

"Your boasting is not good. Do you not know that a little yeast leavens the whole batch?" (1 Corinthians 5:6).

Any kind of leaven, when added to dough and liquids, causes fermentation. Often when leaven is referred to in the Bible, it symbolizes sin, and rightly so. Like leaven, sin is pervasive, ultimately permeating the entire body of liquid or dough.

You won't find a loaf of bread that is only partly affected by yeast—leaven is either present or it isn't. And you won't find a life that is only partly touched by sin—the sin is either there or it isn't. Spiritual leaven is anything that drains your spiritual strength, anything that is contrary to the Gospel, anything that goes against the life of God in the body of Christ.

In Scripture, unleavened bread symbolizes the absolute purity of God, without any contamination. The grain offerings the Israelites presented to God could not be made with leaven. "No grain offering that you bring to the LORD shall be made with leaven, for you shall not burn leaven nor any honey as a food offering by fire to the LORD" (Leviticus 2:11).

During the Festival of Unfermented Cakes, which took place for seven days following the Passover celebration, nothing leavened was permitted in the Israelites' homes:

> Seven days you shall eat unleavened bread. On the first day you shall put away leaven out of your houses, for whoever eats leavened bread from the first day until the seventh day, that person shall be cut off from Israel" (Exodus 12:15).

The Israelite fathers thoroughly searched their homes, took all of the leaven out and burned it. This removal of the leaven symbolically separated the

Israelites from the world. They were told to remove the leaven, and they did it without question.

Leaven always permeates, or spreads throughout, the place it resides, and it has been associated with corruption through the ages. Plutarch, the Greek biographer, spoke of leaven as "the product of corruption. (It) produces corruption in the dough with which it is mixed."[1] One small bit of leaven can contaminate three measures of meal, which made about a bushel of dough. Jesus repeatedly warned His followers to watch out for leaven: "Then Jesus said to them, 'Take heed and beware of the yeast of the Pharisees and Sadducees'" (Matthew 16:6).

When Jesus told His followers to beware of leaven, He was warning against the false doctrine and hypocritical practices of the day. He knew those practices had a corrosive effect on the souls of men. Today, God is calling us to get the leaven out of our lives and move forward into the unleavened bread of holiness!

Leaven, like rust when left to its own devices,

becomes increasingly corrosive until it literally eats its host! Leaven permeates and corrupts whatever it comes in contact with, and God tells us to purge it from every crevice of our lives.

The enemy is no slouch. He continues to patiently gnaw away, deceiving many of God's people into practicing a compromised Gospel, until the Church is pleasingly palatable to everyone, except God. Over the centuries, the Church has changed its dogmas and traditions so completely that now it seldom offends those who hear it – except for God.

The Church of Jesus Christ was born through men and women who did not know the meaning of compromise. Yet, within the Church today we have advocates for abortion, ministers openly in homosexual relationships, believers who don't tithe, people who don't pray, and Christians who never serve.

Eleven apostles were *martyred* for their beliefs, and a twelfth died in prison. How did the Church stray so far from people like these who were willing to sacrifice their very lives for God? Where in the Bible does it say we should dilute the Gospel to please the crowd?

Where in the Word of God are we told to compromise for the sake of congeniality? That's not in my Bible. My Bible says,

> *I know your works, that you are neither cold nor hot. I wish you were cold or hot. So then, because you are lukewarm, and neither cold nor hot, I will spit you out of My mouth. He who has an ear, let him hear what the Spirit says to the churches* (Revelation 3:15-16, 22).

Few people enjoy messages about sin, but sin is the one thing we all have in common. And it's the one thing that stops us from receiving all the good God intends for us.

When there are 200 or more abortions in the United States for every 1,000 live births, it's time for change. When Christian marriages are ending in divorce at nearly the same rate as secular marriages, it's time for change. When men and women walk up and down the streets with no place to lay their heads at night, no blanket to shield themselves from the cold and no food to eat—in the most affluent nation on the planet—it's time for change. When family members victimize children, isn't it time for change?

Are you willing to put away all leaven from your life and to hold your Christian friends and church leaders to the same leaven-free standard? It is time to get the leaven of psychology out of our pulpits and put back the blood-bought Gospel of Jesus Christ. It is time to get Christians out of the comfy pews and into the unsaved streets. We need to share the truth of Jesus Christ with our co-workers, friends, neighbors, and even strangers. It is time for the love and grace of God, because He is watching us. The writer of Hebrews tells us,

> *Therefore, since we are receiving a kingdom that cannot be moved, let us be gracious, by which we may serve God acceptably with reverence and godly fear. For our God is a consuming fire* (Hebrews 12:28-29).

If the Church today would follow this example as a symbolic spiritual directive, and root out leaven from its midst, imagine the joy and power God could pump through us!

LEAVEN AND PRAYERS DO NOT MIX

In one dramatic passage of the Bible, God rebukes transgressing Israel with these words: "Burn leavened bread as a thank offering; announce your voluntary offerings loudly, for so you love to do, O children of Israel, says the Lord GOD" (Amos 4:5).

God was telling the Israelites that all their worship at Bethel and Gilgal was transgression against Him anyway, so they might as well offer leavened bread on the altar and brag about it, because that is what they liked to do. Since all of their offerings were already in vain, they were committing idolatry. God was telling them, in effect, "Your sin is the same as offering Me leavened sacrifices."

When Jesus spotted leaven, He quickly came against it. He boldly denounced the leaven of the Pharisees, calling them hypocrites. Jesus proclaimed that the Pharisees were more concerned with outward show than with the inner condition of their hearts. He pointed out the faulty doctrinal viewpoints of the Sadducees, declaring that their rejection of the resurrection of man was contrary to God's Word. And He exposed the immoral, lustful actions, hypocrisy and political treachery of the followers of Herod.

Paul rebuked the Galatians for allowing the leaven of salvation through works, and reminded them that they were not justified by the law, but by grace. He also warned the church at Corinth about the creeping leaven of malice and wickedness:

Therefore purge out the old yeast, that you may be a new batch, since you are unleavened. For even Christ, our Passover, has been sacrificed for us. Therefore let us keep the feast, not with old yeast, nor with the yeast of malice and wickedness, but with the unleavened bread of sincerity and truth (1 Corinthians 5:7-8).

Paul goes on to tell us not to mix with the fornicators, idolaters, or extortionists of the world. They will pollute our souls as surely as the pinch of leaven that contaminates the entire loaf:

CHAPTER 1 | THE CORROSIVE EFFECTS OF LEAVEN

But I have written to you not to keep company with any man who is called a brother, who is sexually immoral, or covetous, or an idolater, or a reviler, or a drunkard, or an extortioner. Do not even eat with such a person (1 Corinthians 5:11).

It is time for the body of Christ to clear out the unclean, corrupting influence of immorality within our churches. Just as the Israelites would permit absolutely no leaven in their homes during the Festival of Unfermented Cakes, God wants no leaven in our hearts:

For we, through the Spirit, by faith, eagerly wait for the hope of righteousness. For in Christ Jesus neither circumcision nor uncircumcision means anything, but faith which works through love. You were running well. Who hindered you from obeying the truth? This persuasion does not come from Him who calls you. A little yeast leavens the whole batch (Galatians 5:5-9).

WE CANNOT BE MOVED!

In my office I have a 100-year-old volume of *Foxe's Book of Martyrs*. That amazing book describes the following true story:

In Holland, in the year 1527, was martyred and burned a good and virtuous widow, named Wendelmuta. This widow, receiving to her heart the brightness of God's grace, by the appearing of the Gospel, was apprehended and committed to the Castle of Werden, and shortly after was brought to appear at the general sessions of that country. Several monks were appointed to talk with her, that they might convince her and win her to recant; but she, constantly persisting in the truth, would not be moved. Many also of her kindred tried to reason with her; among whom there was a noble matron, who loved and favoured dearly the widow in prison. This matron coming, and communing with her, said, "My Wendelmuta, why doest thou not keep silence, and think secretly in thine heart these things which thou believest, that thou mayest prolong here thy days in life?[2]

What a tempting idea. Just think secretly those things you know will offend the heathen, and then everything will be all right.

Isn't that what we do today? We sit mutely in our pews while some so-called "Christian" organizations condone sexual intercourse before marriage, allow homosexual and lesbian preachers to occupy pulpits in the name of Jesus, and sit by while ordained ministers contend that Jesus was not born of a virgin and was not resurrected from the dead.

We even encourage our government to keep laws that perpetuate the American holocaust against unborn children. Every taxpayer in America is supporting the abortion industry! In its 2017-2018 annual report Planned Parenthood, the nation's most prolific abortion provider, disclosed that it received more than $560 million in grants and other government payments. That's 34 percent of its income during the period covered by the annual report. Planned Parenthood, in the same report, claimed to have performed 332,757 abortions. That's almost 38 abortions every hour of every day for an entire year—one every 95 seconds!

So, how did Wendelmuta, this precious lady, answer? She began with Scripture.

She answered, 'Ah, you know not what you say. It is written, "For with the heart one believes unto righteousness, and with the mouth confession is made unto salvation" (Romans 10:10).

And thus, remaining firm and steadfast in her belief and confession, on the 20th day of November she was condemned by sentence as an heretic, to be burned to ashes, and her goods to be confiscated; she was taking the sentence of her condemnation mildly and quietly.

After she came to the place where she

was to be executed, a monk had brought out a cross, desiring her to kiss and worship her God. 'I worship,' said she, 'no wooden god, but only that God which is in heaven.'[3] And so with a joyful countenance, she went to the stake.

Then taking the powder, and laying it to her breast, she gave her neck willingly to be bound, and with an ardent prayer commended herself to the hands of God. When the time came that she should be strangled, she modestly closed her eyes, and bowed down her head as one that would take a sleep. The fire then was put to the wood, and she, being strangled, was burned afterwards to ashes, instead of this life to get the immortal crown in heaven.

Who put Wendelmuta to death? The Church! The diluted, ravaged body of a weakened Church, so infested with leaven that it was no longer the Church at all, but a shell of empty, meaningless piety.

Is that the kind of Church you want any part of? Is

the modern-day Church in danger of degenerating into that same infected body of religiosity? Leaven lurks in the darkness like a tempting prostitute, and too many churches are courting it.

Leonard Ravenhill asked,

> How can you take it easy? How can you take it easy with a thousand tribes to tell? How can you take it easy in a world that is bound for hell? How can you take it easy with the church asleep in its ease? How can you take it easy? Would someone tell me, please?[4]

I cry with Leonard Ravenhill. It is time we say, "If we belong to God, then let us show ourselves as God's!" If God shows Himself as God, and we are convinced of His Lordship, then let us abandon ourselves utterly to Him. As Paul wrote to the church at Phillipi:

> *Yes, certainly, I count everything as loss for the excellence of the knowledge of Christ Jesus my Lord, for whom I have forfeited the loss of all things and count them as rubbish that I may gain Christ* (Philippians 3:8).

It's time we join together and cleanse the leaven from the Gospel bridge, and lay down planks sturdy enough to get humanity out of its weakened existence and into the powerful presence of God. All leaven must go!

When the Church gets right, we will see all of Isaiah's power and prophetic insight, all of Jeremiah's fury, all of Hosea's love, all of Daniel's victory, all of Peter's power, and all of Paul's revelations. The very power that was manifested in Christ will be brought together and released on this planet in a mighty deluge of God's glory! It is the Church's birthright. It's what God wants for His children.

REACH OUT AND TAKE IT!

When powerful truths have been weakened, it is our responsibility to restore them. Foundational Biblical realities—the cornerstones upon which God Himself is building a Church—must be proclaimed once again.

Let us get into the holy Word of God and pray for a spirit of wisdom and revelation to ring out across this great nation and around the world! Nothing can stop revival once the Church gets this down. Nothing can stop the outpouring of the Holy Ghost. Nothing can stop the signs and wonders that will follow those who minister in the name of Jesus! As our Lord tells us, much as He told one of His disciples: "And I tell you that you are Peter, and on this rock I will build My church, and the gates of Hades shall not prevail against it" (Matthew 16:18).

It is time to move away from comfortable religion, and to begin walking in the grace of the Spirit that invaded the borrowed tomb of Joseph of Arimathaea, raised up the three-day dead body of the Prince of God and broke the chains of hell and death.

We are to lead others to this truth. We are the John the Baptists of our generation. What a glorious honor, to announce that the Kingdom of God is at hand!
The Bible says that in the last days false prophets shall arise and proclaim Christ as other than He really is. We should expect nothing less. But let them declare their false truths. We will not be deceived if the Spirit leads us! As Paul wrote to the churches in Rome, *"And hope does not disappoint, because the love of God is shed abroad*

in our hearts by the Holy Spirit who has been given to us" (Romans 5:5).

It is time for us go up to the mountain of God, where there is quaking, where the presence of God is overwhelming, and where God will reveal Himself to us. God will give us an ear to hear the true prophets, and we will no longer question or wonder what the truth is.

God wants us to change and mature. He wants His Word to come forth as a prophetic anointing and power to change the world! As surely as the sun came up this morning, the greatest revival we have ever seen or heard of or read about is being birthed, right now! Are you ready for it?

It is our turn for revival, and there will never be a day like the one that is dawning. It is time to repair and restore the broken vessels in the body of Christ. This is our hour. This is our day. The curtain on the scene of life is not going down, it is coming up!

You and I have been chosen by God to be His participants in the final drama of the ages. There will be no greater days than these that are dawning in this end-time generation! Jesus promises you and me, "Truly, truly I say to you, he who believes in Me will do the works that I do also. And he will do greater works than these, because I am going to My Father" (John 14:12).

CHAPTER 2

THE LEAVEN OF THE PHARISEES

They do all their works to be seen by men. They make their Scripture boxes broad and lengthen the tassels on their prayer shawls. They love the places of honor at feasts, and the prominent seats in the synagogues, and greetings in the marketplaces, and being called 'Rabbi' by men (Matthew 23:5-7).

The leaven of the Pharisees consists of everything that is phony in religion. Instead of a deep commitment from the heart, the Pharisees exhibited only the external, outward signs of religiosity.

The Pharisees performed all of the rituals required by law. They fasted twice each week. They tithed faithfully and precisely. They prided themselves on their righteousness, yet they were self-righteous. They looked down on the common people and strived to impress the world with their own outward show.

The Pharisees sought prominence and flattering titles; they even expanded the fringed borders of their prayer shawls for all to see. This would be the same as someone lugging around a big, fat family Bible today, or some other pretentious show of religiosity, everywhere they went. The Pharisees were legalistic and proper to the letter of the law on the outside.

But on the inside, their hearts were not righteous, neither were they holy or clean. Jesus said of these people, "For I say to you that unless your righteousness exceeds the righteousness of the scribes and Pharisees, you will in no way enter the kingdom of heaven" (Matthew 5:20).

The Pharisees were biased in their application of the Law, and they made it burdensome for others. They insisted that it the Law be observed according to their own concepts and traditions of the Law. Jesus said of them, "They fasten heavy loads that are hard to carry and lay them on men's shoulders, but they themselves will not move them with their finger" (Matthew 23:4).

The Pharisees majored in the minor areas of faith. They lost sight of the important matters of the heart: justice, mercy, faithfulness and the love of God. Jesus told them,

> Woe to you, scribes and Pharisees, hypocrites! You tithe mint and dill and cumin, but have neglected the weightier matters of the law: justice and mercy and faith. These you ought to have done without leaving the others undone (Matthew 23:23).

Jesus clashed with the Pharisees on the observance of the Sabbath (Matthew 12:1-2), on the adherence to tradition (Matthew 15:1-2) and on His association with sinners, tax collectors and other unsavory characters. They didn't like anything He did or said. The Pharisees assumed that defilement resulted from personal association with persons who did not observe the Law according to the interpretation of the Pharisees. They even found fault with Jesus and His disciples because they didn't practice the traditional ceremony of hand washing. Jesus said of them,

> *For the Pharisees and all the Jews, unless they wash their hands ritually, do not eat, keeping the tradition of the elders. When they come from the market, unless they wash, they do not eat. And there are many other traditions which they have received and observe, such as the washing of cups and pitchers and bronze vessels and dining couches.*
>
> *So the Pharisees and scribes asked Him, "Why do Your disciples not live according to the tradition of the elders, but eat bread with unwashed hands?"*
>
> *He answered, "Well has Isaiah prophesied of you hypocrites, as it is written:*

These people honor Me with their lips, but their hearts are far from Me. In vain do they worship Me,teaching as doctrines the precepts of men.'

For laying aside the commandment of God, you hold the tradition of men—the washing of pitchers and cups, and many other such things you do."

And He said to them, "You full well reject the commandment of God so that you may keep your own tradition"
(Mark 7:3-9).

    Jesus' disciples understood that when He said, "Beware of the leaven of the Pharisees" (Matthew 16:11), He was talking about their doctrine and their practices. Jesus frequently exposed the Pharisees' wrong reasoning and showed them to be violators of God's law because of their adherence to their own man-made traditions.

But rather than glorifying God for the miraculous cures Christ Jesus performed on the Sabbath, the Pharisees were filled with rage over what they believed was His violation of the Sabbath Law. The Pharisees were so spiritually blind, they could not recognize the very Son of God, whom they falsely accused of casting out demons through Satan.

PHARISEES LIVE AMONG US STILL

Modern-day Pharisees are no different. Their lives are filled with long prayers, long faces, long tongues and long ceremonies. Their shallow religiosity continues to hamper the ability of the Church to bring the Gospel to the lost, and it is leading millions away from Christ. Praise God that we have the hindsight of Scripture. It gives us the forewarning of the Holy Spirit about the effects of the leaven of the Pharisees.

Pharisees go to church. But their true religion is an external ritual and ceremony that bypasses the true Gospel of Jesus Christ—the one and only Way to God. Showing up at church is not enough. Basic and misrepresented prayer alone will not move heaven.

All over the world, there are beautifully ornamented churches with multi-colored, stained-glass windows and golden candelabras on marble altars. Yet, many who fill the pews of those churches no longer dance before the Lord. And if they shout at all, it's in the back room. They are losing power and hope. As Paul wrote,

> *(T)eaching us that, denying ungodliness and worldly desires, we should live soberly, righteously, and in godliness in this present world, as we await the blessed hope and the appearing of the glory of our great God and Savior Jesus Christ* (Titus 2:12-13).

It does not matter if the church we attend has a Pentecostal name above the door, a Methodist name, a Baptist name, a Catholic name, or a Presbyterian name. What matters is what burns within our hearts. Decision is reflected by action: coming to the altar, raising our hands to God, and repeating the preacher's words (Pharisees are real good at those). But conversion comes from the heart.

What is in your heart? Do you have a fire in your heart? Do you have an anointing in your heart? Do you have any victory or any power in you? When we have those things in us, we will begin to see cripples stepping out of wheelchairs and the blind regaining their sight. We will begin to see abortion clinics shutting down. We will begin to see pornographers leaving town. Most importantly, we will begin to see hearts convicted of their sin, sincerely repenting, and trusting in God through His Son, Jesus Christ.

I ran to the altar at the age of eight, and my spiritual thirst was quenched with living water. Ever since that time, I have been coming back to the well. When God touched my heart, no one had to drag me back to church the following week. There was no pastoral follow-up visit. No one had to promise me a chicken dinner so I'd return. I was saved to the bone. Hallelujah!

How did I get there? Through the power and conviction of the Holy Spirit. I realized that I was a dirty, rotten, stinking hunk of sinful flesh doomed to an eternity of separation from our gracious and loving God. I heard the preacher tell me that hell is so hot that the fire is never quenched, that hell is a place where men gnaw their tongues to take their minds of the never-ending pain.

When I give an altar call, I don't say, "Run on down here and God will bless your business! Run on down here and all the financial problems you have will disappear! Give your heart to God, and you will experience God's abundant blessing through a bigger house, a better job, obedient children, and a wife who will love you beyond your wildest dreams!"

No. Those are the things Pharisees will tell you. The blessings of God do not come from signing up as a church member, shaking the preacher's hand, smiling with the deacons, or carrying a Bible in public. His blessings come when we kneel at the foot of the Cross of Christ and plead for His blood to wash our sins away and for our name to be recorded in the Lamb's Book of Life! Have you done that? If so, then get ready for true blessings! The apostle John wrote,

They shall bring into it the glory and the honor of the nations. No unclean thing shall ever enter it, nor shall anyone who commits abomination or falsehood, but only those whose names are written in the Lamb's Book of Life (Revelation 21:26-27).

It is time to expose the leaven of the Pharisees in the Church. It is time for preachers to start telling sinners that there is still a King who conquers, a Lord who loves, and a heaven for home. There is still a Holy Spirit who satisfies, and a Christ who is coming again!

Church, let us no longer sit in the doldrums of religious mishmash. We need more than religion, more than seminary training, more than church on Sunday, more than fancy spiritual growth seminars with high-powered, high-paid consultants. We need hope. We need God.

REMEMBER OUR ROOTS

Some of us seem to have forgotten that we were once lost sinners. It is easy for me to rejoice in God's goodness when I remind myself of who I was before I was saved, compared to who I am today. I jump to my feet, clap my hands and shout! I praise His name with all my might when I remember that I was on my way to hell, but now I'm on my way to heaven through the blood of Jesus Christ. That joy comes from the Spirit of the Lord, not the leaven of the Pharisees.

Jesus did not come into this world and die so we could tell a wealthy man, "You're just fine. Come on, sit down right in front here and shake my hand," and then hope he puts in a good offering. We cannot stop teaching the truth of the Gospel out of fear that Mr. Big Bucks might not come back. God's grace is sufficient. If He has begun a good work, He will be faithful to complete it.

We must not be afraid to preach the essential Gospel as Paul wrote to the churches at Rome,

> *For all have sinned and come short of the glory of God, being justified freely by His grace through the redemption that is in Christ Jesus, whom God has set forth to be a propitiation through faith, in His blood, for a*

demonstration of His righteousness, because in His forbearance God had passed over the sins previously committed (Romans 3:23-25).

A preacher once asked me, "How do I get people saved in my church?" "Tell them the truth," I answered. "Tell them that they're sinners and that God wants to cure them."

Another preacher once came up to me and said, "Now, Brother Rod, you don't have to scream into the TV camera that people are sinners—they already know they're sinners." But sadly, many do not know they're sinners, because their pastors are afraid to tell them so. I knew I was a sinner because I had godly parents who prayed for me. They took me to the house of God and taught me about Shadrach, Meschach, and Abednego. They told me about Daniel and the fiery furnace. And about David and his slingshot.

Today, we have a generation of parents who are working for worldly gain at the cost of their family's unity. We lack sin-consciousness. Our congregations are full of people who party all weekend, then go to church on

Sunday. We are ministering to a generation that's been told it's "normal" to sleep around, to abort babies, to rub crystals, to guzzle booze, to do drugs, to think God is a fable, and to live in sexual relationships outside the bonds of marriage.

Our teenagers are sleeping together on Friday night and running down to the altar on Sunday morning. They are not experiencing the power of God in their church to draw them to anything better! Let's give them hope, in our homes and in our churches, for a life full of the blessings and joys of living consecrated to God. They are the future of this great country.

GROWING, OR SLOWING?

At the same time, we need to have compassion for this sin-stricken world. We need to help them understand that God wants us all to grow and to change. If you're still the same as when you accepted the Lord, then you're not growing. Jesus changes lives!

Don't be like little Johnny, who one night fell out of bed in his sleep. When his mother asked him what happened, Johnny replied, "I guess I stayed too close to where I got in." Have you changed since you first accepted Jesus? Or have you stayed close to where you got in?

God aches for us to stop trying to see how close we can live to the world and still be saved! The Holy Spirit cringes and weeps when we snuggle up to the devil. Jesus cries out for us to be convicted of our sinful attitudes and get the leaven of the Pharisees out of our lives.

Conviction is good. It reminds us that we are sinners, and it turns us from our sin. The conviction of God is to our spirit what pain is to our body. Pain is not our enemy; it is the indication that an enemy exists and is invading our territory. Without pain, we could walk down a sandy beach, cut our foot on a jagged bottle and bleed to death.

Let's not let that happen to God's beloved Church. Let us feel the pain of conviction, so the leaven of the Pharisees will not invade our flesh. Let us not walk on in blissful ignorance, while the life-saving blood of Jesus

CHAPTER 2 | THE LEAVEN OF THE PHARISEES

Christ drains from us. Let us not pamper sin! Let us not bow before any golden calf!

Imagine the scene after the Judgment Seat, as people are being dragged kicking and screaming to the lake of fire and brimstone, crying out the names of their preachers and weeping, "Why didn't you tell us the things we were doing would damn our souls? We would have stopped! We would have run from them! You never told us they were wrong; *why didn't you tell us?*"

If we love God's children, we must prevent that from coming to pass! We must root out religious traditionalism before it damns untold millions to hell. Jesus said, "Beware the leaven of the Pharisees." Today, that means we must:

- Beware of the self-proclaimed prophets on television who will pray for us as long as we continue to send them money.
- Beware of volumes of preaching followed by voids of action.

- Beware of great swelling words that lack anointing power.
- Beware of false images of God.

We can go around believing anything about God that we choose to believe. But to believe anything other than what the Bible says is to worship a false image.

THE FINAL GENERATION

Some Christians can be pretty gullible. False prophets come from everywhere, renting out auditoriums, displaying signs that read: "John Doe, Prophet of God."

Too many vulnerable Christians don't take time to study the Bible, don't spend time in their prayer closet, and don't take time to have a relationship with God, but will go to these meetings to get a word from Him! Then they come back home excited and thrilled that someone told them their name. Baloney.

Church members have come to me and said, "Oh, but Brother Rod, this prophet told me my name, man!"

I ask, "Didn't you know your name before you went to the meeting?"

"Well, y-y-y-yes," they stammer with deep conviction and a straight face, "but he told me my address. He told me where I live!"

Hogwash. One Sunday morning I walked into our congregation, approached a lady I had never seen before, and announced her name. She was stunned.

"Have I ever met you before?" I asked.

"No!" she replied, her voice trembling with excitement.

"Then how did I know your name?" I questioned her. Before she could answer, I added, "By the way, you also live at such-and-such address and your phone number is so-and-so."

She almost fell out in the aisle — the ushers had to prop her up. When the hubbub died down, I again spoke with the lady. "Now, ma'am," I asked her, "have I ever met you before?"

"No, Pastor, you have not," she replied, gasping

for breath.

"Then how did I know your name, address and phone number?"

"God must have told you!" she blurted breathlessly.

"Uh-huh, is that right," I said. "Ma'am, will you please look over your shoulder there and tell me what you see?"

She turned and looked and said, "Well, I see a television camera."

"Ma'am," I asked her, "would you please take out your checkbook like you did during the offering?" She took out her checkbook and opened it.

I continued, "Now ma'am, when you were writing out your check, that television camera became my eyes and zoomed in on your name, address and phone number on your check. When the usher walked up here, he handed me a piece of paper on which the television operator had written where you were in the pews, what your name was, and what your address was. The TV camera caught that information, and the usher brought it to me."

CHAPTER 2 | THE LEAVEN OF THE PHARISEES

By this time, that sweet lady was a bit embarrassed. But she was also much wiser. I did not intend to humiliate or confuse that woman. I was illustrating a point: it is critical that we learn to use wisdom and discernment so we are not easily deceived by false prophets.

Do not be deceived. The cameraman is not God. For every true prophet, there will be a false one. The only way the Church can discern the difference is by knowing God.

How can we know God? Get alone, away from all the noise in your life until you are in the very presence of God. Pray in the Holy Ghost. Fast and study God's Word. Then the Holy Spirit will lead you into all truth. Then you will know the Spirit of truth from the spirit of error. The writer of Hebrews admonished us, "But solid food belongs to those who are mature, for those who through practice have powers of discernment that are trained to distinguish good from evil" (Hebrews 5:14).

Be strong! Be sharp! Be accurate! These are not impossible tasks. We are the blessed people of God! We are His final generation! Learn to hear God's voice, and declare His Word to a dying generation.

Church, I beg you: beware of the leaven of the Pharisees. Inside, they are death.

BEYOND MERE PREACHING

The Church frequently calls its evangelistic meetings "revivals," yet few have power or words that revive. True revival rehabilitates, reconstructs, rejuvenates, refreshes, restores, resurrects, renews, and repairs! Paul said, "My speech and my preaching was not with enticing words of man's wisdom, but in demonstration of the Spirit and of power" (1 Corinthians 2:4).

Paul knew that the Gospel was far beyond mere preaching. It was a demonstration of God's power.
The great Lutheran church did not begin because it had a fancy tent, a good-sounding band and brightly colored lights to attract a crowd. It began in the Spirit.
The Pentecostal revival that shook this nation in the early 1900s began in the Spirit.

Revival begins in the Spirit—not with fancy

tricks, air-conditioned churches, empty words, dead ceremonies, or irrelevant rituals. It begins in the Holy Spirit.

If we will go back to the basics of Christianity, if we will stop looking for the next exciting new preacher or a dynamic new denomination, if we will get back to where we began, then God's glory will overtake us, empower us and unleash us! We began in the Spirit, let us finish in the Spirit.

In order for us to become coals of revival, flaming embers filled with the power of God, we must first rebuke the leaven of the Pharisees – false pride, attitudes of separation and superiority, meaningless traditions and superficial rituals that bring forth no fruit. Through the power of the Holy Ghost, we can choose to go forth and reach the lost in a dying world! The question is, will we?

DEDICATION WITHOUT SEPARATION?

"Do not be conformed to this world, but be transformed by the renewing of your mind, that you may prove what is the good and acceptable and perfect will of God" (Romans 12:2).

The only way to understand the will of God is by the renewing of the mind by the transformation that comes as a result of separating from the world and uniting with Him. The Bible tells us God's will, but a mind that has not been renewed cannot understand His will.

Spiritual death is separation from the life flow of God. Believe it or not, there are people who are born again but who are the walking, breathing, talking dead, lacking renewed minds.

To be carnally minded is death, but to be spiritually minded is life and peace, for the carnal mind is hostile toward God, for it is not subject to the law of God, nor indeed can it be, and those who are in the flesh cannot please God (Romans 8:6-8).

Our soul is composed of the mind, the will, and the emotions. When we are born again, our mind is not born again, our will is not born again, and our emotions are not born again. It is only our spirit man that is born again. That is why Paul instructed the Christians at Rome, and by extension us, "I urge you therefore, brothers, by the mercies of God, that you present your bodies as a living sacrifice, holy, and acceptable to God, which is your reasonable service of worship" (Romans 12:1).

To be "carnally minded" does not mean we spiritually cease to exist. It means we exist apart from God's life flow. We are robbed of our joy, our peace, our righteousness, and our relationship with the Father. The Cross of Christ has broken the power of carnality. It is time for the Church to stop allowing a carnal mind to dominate us. If you are sick and tired of the enemy batting your mind back and forth as he pleases, then choose to stand up for righteousness, take control of the carnal nature and be delivered from those bondages.

From Genesis to Revelation, Jesus said, "The words I say are spirit. They are life." His Words will drive death and the grave out of the body, the mind, and the spirit. His Words are alive! "In Him was life, and the life was the light of mankind. The light shines in darkness, but the darkness has not overcome it" (John 1:4-5).

What we do for God is not nearly as important as

what is done by God. It is not the programs, propaganda, pep rallies or perky personnel that count. Rather, it is God's power at work in us, through us, and for us to His glory!

FOUR SIMPLE THINGS

To grow in maturity and to discern the Spirit of truth, we need to do four simple things:

- Fast.
- Pray.
- Study God's Word.
- Kneel at the foot of the Cross of Christ and plead for His crimson blood to wash our sins away.

When we do these things, we will begin to recognize that in order for us to enter into the Spirit of the Lord and to be freed once and for all from the spirit of the world, we must first join a spiritual revolution against the leaven of the Pharisees.

CHAPTER 2 | THE LEAVEN OF THE PHARISEES

Jesus said during His return to His boyhood home of Nazareth,

The Spirit of the Lord is upon Me, because He has anointed Me to preach the gospel to the poor; He has sent Me to heal the broken-hearted, to preach deliverance to the captives and recovery of sight to the blind, to set at liberty those who are oppressed; to preach the acceptable year of the Lord (Luke 4:18-19).

We are all called to bring the Gospel to the poor; to bring deliverance to those addicted to drugs and alcohol; to remove the blinders from the eyes of atheists, abortion advocates, homosexuals and all others who are separated from God; and to minister to all who are hurting and abused. That will not happen until we get the leaven of the Pharisees out of the Church and out of our own lives. How can we start getting the leaven out?

We begin with fasting. Fasting is not just physical abstinence from food. Many in the body of Christ have not been taught the function and importance of fasting. Some almost seem to think fasting is a sort of spiritual hunger strike to force God's hand. That's probably a good way to die; because God is not all that impressed by our meager portion sizes. It makes little difference to Him whether we have one or two cheeseburgers.

What He cares about is when we deny the natural man and bring our body and soul into submission to our spirit man. This allows us to hear what God is trying to say to us, and it helps Him conform us to the will and the image of His Son.

We do not fast from food (or from television, golf, or Sunday afternoon football) to change God's mind. We cannot change the mind of God by fasting. We do, however, move God by faith: the steadfast confidence, trust, and assurance in the fact that God says what He means, means what He says, and will back up His Word.

Fasting is the denial of the natural man. It is a process of purification that disciplines our carnal nature. That is why we fast. It helps loose the bands of wickedness, undoes the heavy burdens, lets the oppressed go free, and breaks every yoke.

Once the natural man has been brought into submission to the spirit man, then we can begin to walk in the reality of the following verse:

> *Is it not to divide your bread with the hungry and bring the poor who are outcasts into your house? When you see the naked, to cover him and not hide yourself from your own flesh?* (Isaiah 58:7).

"To divide your bread with the hungry" means to be willing to sacrifice what we have to help those in need. It means being willing to stop walking around in our beautiful, clean robes, pretending everything is wonderful, and instead step into our jeans and hard hats, take a walk in the mud of life, and extend ourselves for the children of God.

When we start to function in accordance with verse 7 of Isaiah 58, then we qualify to claim God's promises in verses 8 and 9:

Then your light shall break forth as the morning, and your healing shall spring forth quickly, and your righteousness shall go before you; the glory of the LORD shall be your reward. Then you shall call, and the LORD shall answer; you shall cry, and He shall say, Here I am.

A study of this passage shows that in less time than it takes our minds to send an impulse to our tongues to speak His Name, He has already answered! God is looking for those who are ready to join Him on the front line, to obey His Word, and to receive His blessings.

God says, "If you do not deal your bread to the hungry, if you do not clothe the naked, if you do not take care of the disadvantaged, if you do not turn your face from the naked and cover them, and if you do not minister to those in need, then you will walk in darkness and your health will not spring forth." That is what the Bible says! And He is clear: only through obedience to His Word can we receive the blessings He has promised us!

Some people are never sick because they "divide their bread" every day: at missions, at inner-city outreaches, at food and clothing pantries and at homeless shelters.

The leaven of the Pharisees shuns the sick, avoids the poor, walks across the street from the downtrodden, and loves money. The blood-bought Church of Jesus Christ gives money away to warm the back of someone who is cold, and to put food in the belly of someone who has not eaten for days. That is a Gospel the Pharisees just didn't get.

Today, God is challenging us to exchange the leaven of the Pharisees for the love of the good Samaritan. He is challenging us to sow into the lives of the disadvantaged, to clothe the naked, to bring food to the hungry.

Now is the hour for the Church to thank God for the opportunity to divide our bread. Now is the hour for us to joyfully and liberally sow our seed in order to spread the Gospel. Now is the hour for healing to be manifested in the incredible power of the full light of God. Now is the hour for us to declare, "The leaven of the Pharisees shall be rooted out, once and for all."

The Church is not just a building in which to worship. The Church is a caring body of believers who reach out to the hurting and the desperate, to help people who do not have enough food or clothes, to go to those who need the ministering touch of the saints, and to minister to people who desperately need a Church that is free of the leaven of the Pharisees and who will love them joyfully and unconditionally.

There are three kinds of people in this world:
• Those who make good things happen.
• Those who watch things happen.
• And those who wonder what happened!

Which are you? Are you the good Samaritan? Or are you a Pharisee, who would cross to the other side to avoid people in their time of need?

From now on a crown of righteousness is laid up for me, which the Lord, the righteous Judge, will give me on that Day, and not only to me but also to all who have loved His appearing (2 Timothy 4:8).

Today's church must live by the Word of God, and empty itself of the leaven of the Pharisees! We must know that He will return at any moment. What would you like to be doing the instant you hear His voice?

CHAPTER 3

THE LEAVEN OF THE SADDUCEES

"For the Sadducees say that there is no resurrection, nor angel, nor spirit. But the Pharisees acknowledge them all" (Acts 23:8).

The Sadducees were prominent in Jewish society during the time of Jesus Christ. A religious sect, like the Pharisees, the Sadducees also opposed Jesus and His disciples. However, the Sadducees also rejected all things "supernatural." This meant that they denied the resurrection from the dead and the existence of angels.

To try to catch Jesus in a theological quandary concerning the existence of the resurrection, the Sadducees created a scenario of a woman who had successively married her six brothers-in-law after her original husband died. The Saducees thought their analytical dilemma would stump Jesus on the theological question of the resurrection, and, therefore, of heaven itself:

> *The same day the Sadducees, who say that there is no resurrection, came to Him and asked Him, "Teacher, Moses said, 'If a man dies having no children, his brother must marry his wife and raise up children for his brother.' Now there were seven brothers with us. The first died after he married and, having no children, left his wife to his brother. Likewise the second and third, on to the seventh. Last of all, the woman died also. Therefore, in the resurrection, whose wife shall she be of the seven? For they all had her* (Matthew 22:23-28).

Jesus recognized that the Sadducees were attempting to mock him publicly and trick Him theologically. He silenced them by quoting the very Scriptures that the Sadducees themselves professed to study. "Jesus answered, 'You err, not knowing the Scriptures nor the power of God. For in the resurrection they neither marry nor are given in marriage, but are like the angels of God in heaven'" (Matthew 22:29-30).

Jesus did not stop with the explanation that there would not be marriages in heaven. Knowing the hypocritical nature of the Sadducees, He also refuted their rejection of the resurrection of the dead:

> *But concerning the resurrection of the dead, have you not read what was spoken to you by God, 'I am the God of Abraham, the God of Isaac, and the God of Jacob?' God is not the God of the dead, but of the living* (Matthew 22:31-32).

The Sadducees accepted only the Pentateuch (the first five books of the Old Testament) as valid Scripture. So they rejected the idea of a resurrection, because they could find no evidence in their Scriptures to verify such doctrine. However, when Jesus quoted Exodus 3:6, telling them that God Himself says, "I am [not "I was"] the God of Abraham, the God of Isaac, and the God of Jacob," the

Sadducees were silenced from all further attempts to trick Jesus.

The Sadducees rejected much of Scripture as invalid, and they failed to keep God's law. If they wanted to get anywhere near the Kingdom of God, it was necessary for them to produce fruit befitting repentance. The "fruit" they produced instead was based on works, and not on repentance grounded in faith.

The Sadducees' teaching was dangerous because it was contrary to the Word of God. By refusing to believe in heaven, hell, angels, and the resurrection, the Sadducees ignored the clear Word of God and set an example of living contrary to Scripture.

Another characteristic of the Sadducees was that they chose to keep their treasures on earth, and ignored the reality of heaven. Jesus admonished against such practices in the Sermon on the Mount, saying:

> *Do not store up for yourselves treasures on earth where moth and rust destroy and where thieves break in and steal. But store up for yourselves treasures in heaven, where neither*

CHAPTER 3 | THE LEAVEN OF THE SADDUCEES

moth nor rust destroy and where thieves do not break in nor steal, for where your treasure is, there will your heart be also (Matthew 6:19-21).

Christ also warned people about the Sadducees' polluted teaching, comparing it to leaven. He made it clear that He was not referring to the leaven of mere bread:

Then Jesus said to them, "Take heed and beware of the yeast of the Pharisees and Sadducees. How is it that you do not understand that I spoke to you not concerning bread, but that you should beware of the yeast of the Pharisees and Sadducees?" Then they understood that He did not tell them to beware of the yeast of bread, but of the teaching of the Pharisees and Sadducees (Matthew 16:6, 11-12).

The Sadducees were so opposed to the teachings of Christ that after His death and resurrection they were at the forefront of attempts to stop the spread of Christianity. However, the threats of the Sadducees did nothing to stop the apostles' mission of telling people about Jesus.

Jesus knew the Sadducees were liars, and that they desperately needed to know the truth of the Gospel. That is why He so clearly told them, in many different ways, that there is a price to pay for sin, and that price would be extracted for all eternity.

ONE LUCID MOMENT

There was once an old beggar named Lazarus who sat each day at the gate of a rich man, hoping for some of the crumbs that fell from the rich man's table. But the rich man was embarrassed by the presence of the beggar and never lifted a hand to help him. When the wealthy man's friends came by, they would say to him, "You should do something about that poor beggar out there by your gate. It's embarrassing to see him when I come to visit you."

The Bible tells us the rest of that rich man's story. He wound up in hell after he died. He cried out to Abraham: "I am tormented in these flames, but I see over in Abraham's bosom that old beggar man named Lazarus who laid by my gate every day. Please, please go and tell him to dip the tip of his finger in some water and touch it to my tongue. I am in torment because of these flames!"

> But Abraham said, "Son, remember that you in your lifetime received your good things, and Lazarus in like manner evil things. But now he is comforted and you are tormented. And besides all this, between us and you there is a great gulf, so that those who would pass from here to you cannot, nor can those from there pass to us" (Luke 16:25-26).

In England there are little animals called moles. Their fur is used to make beautiful garments. Any time you want, you can just walk into a field and pick up a mole. Why? Because moles are born blind; they spend their entire lives in darkness. They can't see to run away from you.

Since moles' eyes are closed, they don't sense danger unless they are jolted sharply upon the head.

When that occurs, the instant before a mole dies, a strange thing happens: for the first time in their existence, for a brief moment before they pass into death, their eyes open!

    The Sadducees were the dark-dwelling moles of Jesus' day. They did not believe in eternity. They did not believe in heaven or hell. They did not believe in God and the infallibility of His Word. They did not believe in the Son of God and His Church.

    Do you know people like that today? Unless we reach the modern-day Sadducees with the hope of the Gospel, one sad day they are going to get their sudden jolt. Their eyes are going to open wide, and they are going to realize for one lucid moment that the Bible is true, infallible, and inerrant. They are going to recognize that God does exist, He has all along, and they have been deceived by the devil.

    That one lucid moment will come too late. It will come after they die, when they meet God face to face and their sentence is handed down.

    But it is not God's desire to pronounce that

sentence on anyone. He loves them with the same love with which He loves the born-again believer. Our charge is to bring that love to the Sadducees we find in our lives!

THE GREAT TRANSGRESSION

The Sadducees presumed to know more about the nature of God than God Himself. They claimed, contrary to Scripture, that man would not face an eternal resurrection. They claimed, contrary to Scripture, that angels did not exist. They claimed, contrary to Scripture, that Jesus the Messiah Himself was a false prophet. Beware the leaven of the Sadducees. It contains the deadly poison of a viper.

David once asked God to deliver him from the great transgression, pleading: "Keep back Your servant also from presumptuous sins; may they not rule over me. Then I will be upright and innocent from great transgression" (Psalm 19:13).

What was that great transgression? David had committed adultery with Bathsheba, but that was not the great transgression.

David was a murderer—he had Uriah, Bathsheba's husband, killed in a battle where he, as a king, should have been fighting as well. But that was not the great transgression.

There is a transgression, a sin, which is greater than adultery or murder. David's great transgression was the sin of presumption: he arrogantly assumed things about God that weren't true. That was the same trap that snared the Sadducees, who presumed they knew more about what God meant than what He said!

Many people today worship at the golden calf of their own philosophy. They worship at the feet of "intellectualism." They build gods to themselves and say, "This is who God really is. This is how God really responds." How presumptuous.

There should be no conjecture when it comes to the things of God. He gave us a Bible with 66 books in it that declare, "This is who I am and how I respond. Study this book to know Me." As Paul wrote to the Christians at Rome, "For whatever was previously written was written for our instruction, so that through perseverance and encouragement of the Scriptures we might have hope" (Romans 15:4).

To those who remain outside the knowledge of Christ, we need to get the word that the days grow short—though there is still hope. We need to reach out to the deceived of this world:

- To married people who think God will overlook their adulterous affairs.
- To singles who think God will overlook their sexual indiscretions.
- To homosexuals who think God will overlook their transgressions.
- To the 'good people' in our neighborhoods and businesses who think God will be impressed with their works.

We need to declare that the God who made a way for them to have eternal fellowship with Him also will not tolerate anything less than total devotion to Him. As Paul wrote to the church at Corinth,

Do you not know that the unrighteous will not

inherit the kingdom of God? Do not be deceived. Neither the sexually immoral, nor idolaters, nor adulterers, nor male prostitutes, nor homosexuals, nor thieves, nor covetous, nor drunkards, nor revilers, nor extortioners will inherit the kingdom of God* (1 Corinthians. 6:9-10).

In their presumption, the religious Sadducees of our day have put their Jesus in blue jeans and a T-shirt and sent Him strolling to the neighborhood mall shopping for the latest name-brand kicks, leather jacket and hair gel, so He'll look cool after His workout at the gym.

Uh-huh. Is that the Jesus you want—just one of the guys, no different than your friends or co-workers? That's not the Jesus I know. The Jesus I know is a bleeding, dying, resurrecting, life-giving, life-changing, blind-man-healing, leper-cleansing Jesus—a Jesus who leaps through time and space into the fiery trials of life and catches us before the crackling flames touch our soul!

In our wildest imagination we will never be able

to conjure up a more loving, powerful, dynamic, gentle, exciting, awesome Jesus than the Jesus of the Bible!

AMERICA'S GOD?

Time magazine, once one of the great journalistic outlets in our nation, years ago published an article titled, "The Baby Boom Goes Back to Church,"[1] referring to my generation. And history is repeating itself! Thanks in part to the public ministry of my daughter, Ashton, I see more and more millennials in the pews when I preach across the nation.

I'm glad Americans are going back to church, but I'm concerned about who they're going to find when they get there. I'm not confident that they are truly searching for the Jesus of the Bible. My hunch is that they've been duped into looking for a comfortable Jesus—a Jesus who is going to pamper them, put them over the top in their business, heal their body, pop up on the primrose path of material blessing and give them goodies like a spiritual Santa.

Need a new car? Here you go. New boat? No problem. Bigger home? More money? It's yours for the asking!

That kind of Jesus sounds wonderful, but that's not the Jesus of the Bible and it's not the Jesus I serve. The Jesus I serve declares, *"If anyone will come after Me, let him deny himself, and take up his cross, and follow Me"* (Matthew 16:24).

In today's fast-food society, denying oneself isn't something the modern "undercover" Christian wants in a Lord. They hide safely in the sanctuary of their church, shouting, "Bless me, bless me, bless me!" They want the gain without the pain—the glory without the guts. They can't accept that a "loving God" would ever want to allow them to experience tough times.

Well, I have news: experiencing and overcoming tough times is one of the ways God trains us up, builds us, strengthens us and makes us into men and women who can weather any storm. When we are refined in the fires of life, we learn He alone is our source and we place our hope and faith in God. Paul wrote,

CHAPTER 3 | THE LEAVEN OF THE SADDUCEES

Not only so, but we also boast in tribulation, knowing that tribulation produces patience, patience produces character, and character produces hope. And hope does not disappoint, because the love of God is shed abroad in our hearts by the Holy Spirit who has been given to us (Romans 5:3-5).

If you want to know who He is, He is defined in His myriad of names:

- "I am Jehovah Ropheka, the God that healeth thee."
- "I am Jehovah Tsidkenu, the Lord God, your righteousness."
- "I am Jehovah M'kaddesh, the Lord God, your holiness."
- "I am Jehovah Shammah, the God who is always present with you."
- "I am Jehovah Shalom, the God of your peace."
- "I am Jehovah Rohi, the Lord God your shepherd."
- "I am Jehovah Jireh, the God who supplies before there is a need."

Jesus says to you and to me, "I am the lion of the tribe of Judah. I was conceived in the virgin womb of a young girl named Mary. I was conceived of the very Spirit of the living God. I plunged into time from eternity—both of which I created. I came to earth for this reason: to save my people from their sins. That is the reason I am here."

THEY'RE NOT THE 10 'GUIDELINES'

Do you notice how seldom people talk about the Ten Commandments anymore? Some people honestly believe the Ten Commandments don't apply to New Covenant believers! The difference between the Old Covenant and the New Covenant is that God gave us the Law in the Old Covenant, but we didn't have the power to keep it. In the New Covenant, He fulfilled the Law by giving us power to keep it. But modern Sadducees have watered the Ten Commandments down to "Thou shalt not, generally . . ." or Thou shalt not, unless . . ." or Thou shalt not, except . . ."

How is this different than the original Sadducees ignoring or rewriting Scripture to fit their agenda and their desires? What gives us the right to change the Ten Commandments? The very finger of God wrote them:

"When He had made an end of communing with him on Mount Sinai, He gave Moses the two tablets of testimony, tablets of stone, written with the finger of God" (Exodus 31:18).

What Moses brought down from the mountain were not mere guidelines we may wish to consider as a basis for everyday living. They are commands of the God who created the earth, and you and me. Contrary to the teachings of modern-day Sadducees, we are to honor these laws and live by them:

1. "I am the LORD, your God, who brought you out of the land of Egypt, from the house of bondage. You shall have no other gods before Me" (Deuteronomy 5:6-7). That means no other god—not the god of business, not the god of finance, not the god of achievement, not the god of social life, not the god of alcohol or drug abuse, not the god of religion, and certainly not the god of the Sadducees. The only God we can have before us is the God of the Old and New Testaments, the God who is the same yesterday, today, and forever.

2. "You shall not make yourself any graven image, or any likeness of anything that is in heaven above, or that is in the earth beneath, or that is in the waters beneath the earth" (Deuteronomy 5:8). We do not worship golden calves. We do not worship false images. The Sadducees bow down and pay allegiance to false gods, while Jehovah God sits on His heavenly throne, "visiting the iniquity of the fathers on the children, and on the third and fourth generations of those who hate Me, but showing mercy to thousands of them that love Me and keep My commandments" (Deuteronomy 5:9b-10).

3. "You shall not take the name of the LORD your God in vain, for the LORD will not exonerate anyone who takes His name in vain" (Deuteronomy 5:11). We all understand that this commandment means that we are not to utter any profanity; that is, we are not to swear or use vulgar language. But there is more to it than that.

CHAPTER 3 | THE LEAVEN OF THE SADDUCEES

The Bible tells us:

> *These signs will accompany those who believe: In My name they will cast out demons; they will speak with new tongues; they will take up serpents; if they drink any deadly thing, it will not hurt them; they will lay hands on the sick, and they will recover* (Mark 16:17-18).

If we believe in the name of Jesus and do not take His name in vain, then we must also cast out devils. The Word of God is not a smorgasbord, where we can pick and choose to believe or follow what suits our fancy, and reject or ignore what doesn't.

When we disagree with the Word of God, we are taking His Name in vain.

Jesus said these signs shall follow us when we believe: we will cast out devils, we will speak with new tongues, we will lay hands on the sick. But too often I hear, "Well now, Brother Rod, I just don't believe in laying hands on people. We just don't do it, and I don't believe God expects us to."

That is a lie that too many church leaders, preachers, teachers, and seminaries are putting into our presumptuous, intellectual minds. Those lies did not come from The Book. I have my degrees hanging up on the wall, but I long ago stopped putting any stock in them because God is beyond our minds. He is beyond our finite capacity to understand Him and His ways.

We were never called to intellectualize God. We were never called to explain God. We were never called to rationalize God. He is not to be understood—He is to be exalted!

One of the greatest profanities for Christians is to take His name but refuse to call on His name. We file into church, go through all the motions, go through our little religious ceremonies, soothe our consciences, then go out just as depressed, just as sick, just as lonely, just as hopeless as when we came in. Is that any type of example of Christianity to a skeptical world?

Don't our children have a right to see an

outpouring of the demonstration of a living God—a God who is not just an idea floating around out there, but is a real God?

The problem is not the atheist shaking his fist in the face of God and proclaiming, "God does not exist." The problem is not the agnostic who says, "Well, there may be a God out there, but He doesn't care about us." The problem is the so-called Christian who, despite the outward facade of Christianity, is a virtual stranger to the character and nature of the God they claim to know and to serve! They have a form of godliness, but they deny His power in their lives! They, more than anyone else, take the name of our precious Lord in vain.

4. "Keep the Sabbath day, to keep it holy, just as the LORD your God has commanded you. Six days you shall labor and do all your work, but the seventh day is the Sabbath of the LORD your God. On it you shall not do any work" (Deuteronomy 5:12-14a). Thou shalt not wax thy car on the Sabbath day. Thou shalt not use the Sabbath day

as the day for shopping or cutting the lawn. The Sabbath is not thine, but God's day! Not just from 10 a.m. until noon, but all day. Time with Him is a gift to us! It's that day when we can relax with our Father, to worship Him and enjoy His attention in our busy, cluttered world. Every Sunday should be our Father's day.

5. "Honor your father and your mother, just as the LORD your God has commanded you, that your days may be prolonged, and that it may go well with you in the land which the LORD your God is giving you" (Deuteronomy 5:16). Did God say, "Honor your parents until you turn 13 or until you no longer agree with their rules?" No. He said to honor them, period. That means all the way up through their last breath on Earth. And by fulfilling this commandment, God promises us that our "days may be long and it may be well with us in the place where we live."

6. "You shall not murder" (Deuteronomy 5:17). This means what it says—we are not to unjustly deprive anyone of his or her life! Suicide is not allowed, according to God's law. Abortions are not allowed, according to God's law (yet unborn babies are being slaughtered at the rate of one every 95 seconds in this nation!). The leaven of the Sadducees has permeated and polluted one of the clearest mandates of God.

7. "You shall not commit adultery" (Deuteronomy 5:18). Today, adultery is considered such a harsh word by many that it is seldom used anymore, even in pulpits. We hear of an "affair," an "indiscretion," a "sexual liaison." There is no delicate way to describe it: adultery is when a married person has sex with someone other than his or her spouse.

Adultery is sin. Jesus broadened the definition of adultery even further, when He said it could also be committed in the heart: "You have heard that it was said by the ancients, 'You shall not commit adultery.' But I say to you that whoever looks on a woman to lust after her has committed adultery with her already in his heart" (Matthew 5:27-28).

8. "You shall not steal." (Deuteronomy 5:19). Do you fudge a little bit on your income tax returns? That is stealing. It is the leaven of the Sadducees that reasons, "I can cheat the government and not pay them the legal amount I owe because it's my hard-earned money they're wasting." But is that the response God tells us to make? "Then Jesus answered them, 'Render to Caesar the things that are Caesar's, and to God the things that are God's.' And they were amazed at Him" (Mark 12:17).

You may have noticed, Jesus did not add, "Unless, of course, they prove themselves to be slovenly money managers; in that case, I would advise you to go ahead and rip them off." No! "Do not steal"

CHAPTER 3 | THE LEAVEN OF THE SADDUCEES

means to render to the rightful owner those things that do not belong to you. It also means to give an honest day's work for an honest day's wages. Some Christians expect God or the local trade union to miraculously promote them, regardless of their work ethic. Let's put our reliance back on God.

If we will work hard, as if God Himself is our employer, then He will bless the work of our hands. If we would only get the leaven of the Sadducees out of the work ethic of America, we would again surpass the foreign competition, as we did all during the first half of the last century. America was founded on good, hard work, and it is time we get back to the standard of a good day's work for a day's wages. God wants us to be accountable, to be a people of our word, to give a day's work for a day's pay. In actuality, we work for God! Would you like to have

to explain to God *why you've been cheating Him?*

9. "You shall not bear false witness against your neighbor" (Deuteronomy 5:20). Why is it that gossip and rumors run rampant in churches today? Because they're cooking with leaven! A church free of "false witnesses" is a place of warmth, comfort, security, and trust. To the hurting and downtrodden, the Church should represent a sanctuary of safety, a spiritual hospital that specializes in healing, not hurting, those in desperate need of the love of God.

10. *"You shall not covet your neighbor's wife, nor shall you covet your neighbor's house, his field, his male servant, his female servant, his ox, his donkey, or anything that belongs to your neighbor"* (Deuteronomy 5:21). This is one of the most violated commandments of our generation. If we were to root out the leaven of lust, there would be no more pornography hidden in the homes of church ushers, no more "swimsuit issues" on the coffee tables of pastors, no more

"pay-per-view" movie channels bringing filth into the homes of deacons.

This commandment not only deals with those things, but also with our appetite for titles, promotions, recognition, being "lifted up" above our neighbor in our jobs, our service in the church, or our social standing in some service club. Do you know of someone who covets someone else's job? Their house? Their material possessions? They are in sin, plain and simple.

OUR NEW CITY

He who was seated on the throne said, "Look! I am making all things new." Then He said to me, "Write, for these words are faithful and true." He said to me, "It is done. I am the Alpha and the Omega, the Beginning and the End. I will give of the spring of the water of life to him who thirsts (Revelation 21:5-6). We are going to a city where there will be no addictions. No tenement buildings. No one without a home. No ambulances, no destruction by fire, no sickness, no aspirin, no morphine, no sedatives for sleep. God will bring the gift of peace to this new city, the new Jerusalem, the city of the great King. No second-class citizens will dwell there, and the leaven of the Sadducees will be a thing of the past.

Ira Stanphill, the great hymn writer of the Church, put it this way: "I've got a mansion just over the hilltop, in that bright land where we will never grow old. And some day yonder we will never more wander, but walk on streets that are purest gold."[2]

Let us be a Church that is anxious to go to that heavenly city 1,500 miles high with walls made of jasper and gates made of a single pearl 300 feet high. We will stroll down heavenly boulevards of gold and drink from the river of life. Our former troubles will all pass away, and standing at the gate of that celestial city will be the resurrected King of Kings and Lord of Lords.

He will say "No longer let your heart be troubled, My child. Let Me wipe the tears from your eyes. In this city there is no weeping, no crying, no sickness, no pain, no death. You are going to joyfully leap forever on My everlasting hills."

God will wipe the tears away from families ravaged by divorce. He will take away the sorrow of child-abuse victims. He will erase the grief of families victimized by gang shootings. A new Jerusalem is coming, where the glory of God will shine upon all who will get the leaven out.

For believers to dwell in the new Jerusalem, all leaven must first be eliminated. In this city, the leaven will be gone. There will be no abominations, no lies, and no defiling of the sacredness of God's little children. Can you picture it? It is coming! As we stay faithful and overcome the leaven, we will inherit this new city, the new Jerusalem.

A CHURCH ON FIRE!

Jesus has clearly declared, "Beware of the leaven of the Sadducees." (see Matthew 16:6). The world has declared that you may formulate your own idea of who and what God is. Reject that leaven! Millions around the world do not believe Jesus is alive today. Reject that leaven!

Beware of the leaven of the modern-day Sadducees. They are the ones who disbelieve the supernatural, teach against the resurrection, deny the gifts of the Holy Ghost, dismiss heaven and hell and ignore the Ten Commandments. Reject that leaven!

"See, I and the children whom the LORD has given me are for signs and for wonders in Israel from the LORD of Hosts who dwells in Mount Zion" (Isaiah 8:18).

We are a Church given to the world to exalt Him with signs and wonders! So stay strong, Christian! Together we will look the devil in the eyes and rebuke him, pull him down from his throne, and exalt the name of Jesus Christ! We believe in the Holy Ghost, a literal heaven and hell, the supernatural, the resurrection of the dead, and the demonstration of the gifts of the Holy Spirit. We are a real, bona-fide, tongue-talking, devil-stomping, Christ-exalting body!

We reject the leaven of the Sadducees. It has no

place in the New Testament Church! Let us recommit to becoming a Church on fire for the true and literal Word of God!

OUR SPECIAL JOURNEY

> *(C)oncerning His Son, Jesus Christ our Lord, who was born of the seed of David according to the flesh and declared to be the Son of God with power, according to the Spirit of holiness, by the resurrection from the dead"* (Romans 1:3-4).

The irrefutable demonstration of the most profound fact concerning the resurrection of Jesus is that He is not here. There is no final resting place of Jesus Christ! He bodily died and He bodily rose. Without the resurrection, Jesus of Nazareth is no more meaningful than Buddha or Confucius. But His bodily resurrection corroborates His claims that He is the Son of God.

The most vicious leaven of the Sadducees was that they did not believe in the resurrection. Such leaven of unbelief in the resurrection still exists today. One group of modern-day Sadducees says, "We might be able to accept the resurrection of Jesus, but we do not believe in that other resurrection, the extraterrestrial journey we are supposed to take up into the sky someday." They reject the rapture of the Church.

Another group of Sadducees of today are those who do not believe that the same God who resurrects from the dead and will rapture the Church, can resurrect their dead finances, their dead marriage, their dead anointing, their dead joy, or their dead hope. Get away from that leaven! Enter into the presence of God! Read His Word and claim His promises—they're for you!

What an awesome God we have! Jesus would have you, right now as you read this book, to declare, "Jesus, I want You to be part of my life more than I want anything else in the world!" Are you willing to declare that?

Then let's claim revival in the Church and in our lives! Let's declare from the housetops, "Jesus, I am not staying bound up one more day! I will study Your Word to show myself approved, and I will not change one iota of your Word! You are God! I thank you for giving me Your

Word and Your Holy Spirit so that I can grow to know who You truly are! And Lord, I repent of putting false gods before You, and I vow to cleanse the leaven of the Sadducees from my life!"

CHAPTER 4

THE LEAVEN OF THE HERODIANS

"He warned them, 'Take heed. Beware of the yeast of the Pharisees and the yeast of Herod'" (Mark 8:15).

The leaven of the Herodians is the spirit of the world—the lust of the flesh, the lust of the eye.

King Herod exemplified leaven. He was unscrupulous, immoral, cruel, deceitful, cunning and cold-blooded. Because of his shameless lifestyle, Herod was eventually afflicted with a repugnant disease. Josephus, the Jewish historian, describes Herod's affliction: "An intolerable itching over all the surface of his body . . . continual pains in his colon . . . dropsical tumors about his feet . . . an inflammation of the abdomen . . . a purification that produced worms. Besides which he had a difficulty of breathing upon him, and could not breathe but when he sat upright, and had a convulsion of all his members."

The world was Herod's playground, and he wallowed in it like rot in a cesspool. He had absolutely no moral integrity, and the spirit of lust ruled him. The Bible tells us that he even married his own sister-in-law, Herodias (the wife of his brother Philip). When the marriage was about to take place, John the Baptist boldly admonished the king that he was violating the Word of God in marrying his brother's wife. Following the lust of his flesh, Herod married Herodias anyway, ignoring God's law as well as the warning of the prophet John. On Herod's birthday, his young stepdaughter (the daughter of Herodias, and possibly his brother's daughter—which would have made the girl Herod's own niece) danced for him, and her allure so enticed him that he tried to seduce her with an unheard-of gift:

> *When the daughter of Herodias came in and danced and pleased Herod and those*

who sat with him, the king said to the girl, "Ask of me whatever you desire, and I will give it to you." And he swore to her, '"Whatever you ask of me, I will give you, up to half of my kingdom" (Mark 6:22-23).

Both pride and lust had gripped Herod's heart in trying to entice this young girl with his riches. He no doubt assumed that she would ask for some treasure and that, in his giving it to her, she would feel a great sense of debt to him, which he would take advantage of as he pleased. But to Herod's utter shock, the stepdaughter, who had been prepared for this opportunity by her mother Herodias, didn't ask for riches at all: "Being previously instructed by her mother, she said, 'Give me John the Baptist's head on a platter'" (Matthew 14:8).

Herod's twisted mind must have been reeling! Now, he was not only prevented from carrying out his scheme to take advantage of his young stepdaughter, while making his guests think he was a generous man, but he was also put on the spot to murder a man whose death he knew would gain him nothing but trouble!

Herod had been completely outfoxed. He could have refused his stepdaughter's request—after all, he was the king. He could have had the heads of mother and daughter instead. But Herod was a man of pride. He had made his foolish oath in the presence of several officials and notable dinner guests, and his pride would not allow him to back down from his promise to give his dancing stepdaughter "whatsoever she would ask."

So Herod salvaged his twisted pride by turning the situation into an opportunity to appear powerful, magnanimous and unconcerned. He gave the girl what her mother told her to ask for: "He sent and beheaded John in the prison. His head was brought on a platter and given to the girl, and she brought it to her mother" (Matthew 14:10-11).

What a stunning display of evil! Is it any wonder that Jesus warned His followers about the leaven of the Herodians?

Jesus said Herod and his followers were hypocrites. He warned His disciples to be on the alert for their devious schemes, and he told them to be vigilant in avoiding such leaven: "He warned them, 'Take heed. Beware of the yeast of the Pharisees and the yeast of Herod'" (Mark 8:15).

HERODIANS OF THE NEW MILLENNIUM

The leaven of the Herodians is abundant in society today, as well as in many churches. People will swear that murder is wrong, but they will think nothing of watching murder and violence take place on television and in movies.

People will bite their tongue before they'll curse; yet they'll go and pay money to sit in a theater and listen to actors curse onscreen.

People will shake their heads and gravely denounce adultery, and then go and watch it in movies and read about it in romance novels. Adultery being committed or adultery being portrayed—what's the difference? It's the same spirit being poured out onto the world. We shouldn't be surprised when adulterous images become adulterous thoughts that transform into adulterous actions.

Even the divorce rate among Christians is the same as in the world. Divorce leaves thousands of innocent Little Leaguers and cheerleaders in the wake of their parents' selfishness and lust.

Society is being overtly encouraged by Satan to fling open these doors of debauchery. We must start taking a stand against this Herodian spirit that is strangling morality out of our consciences.

The Supreme Court has consistently over the past few decades upheld the right to kill babies in their mothers' wombs through abortion and have rebuffed attempts to bring prayer into public schools. In 2003, in the case of Lawrence vs. Texas, the high court announced what amounted to a strong endorsement of gay rights when it issued a ruling that struck down a Texas law against "deviate sex acts." Only three justices dissented (Scalia, Rehnquist and Thomas), while Justice Kennedy apologized that the Court had taken so long to overturn longstanding bans on gay sex. And yet, with few exceptions, the church did little to protest this

CHAPTER 4 | THE LEAVEN OF THE HERODIANS

ruling. Then, in 2015, the court in Obergefell v. Hodges substituted the "wisdom" of the court's majority for overwhelming majorities of voters in more than 30 states and mandated same-sex marriage across the nation.

There is no gentle way to say it: The church is going soft on sin. We are in great danger of sinking into a morass from which there will be no escape if we don't act. We can no longer allow the leaven of the Herodians to get a stranglehold on us. Let's cleanse ourselves of it!

It's high time we stand firm against the spirit of the world, the spirit of sexual perversion, the lust of the flesh, the lust of the eyes, and the pride of life. I shudder at the thought of Christians waking up some day in the future, as if from a long sleep, and suddenly asking, "What happened? How did it all get so bad? How did such blatant sins as abortion, child abuse, homosexuality, prostitution, pornography, substance abuse, and gambling become so firmly rooted in our country and ignored by our Church?" But it could happen if we allow the leaven of the Herodians to continue unchecked, without a response of love from the church.

Vast empires of international power and wealth have lasted far longer than America has been in existence, and yet they ultimately collapsed into debauchery and wickedness. If it could happen to the mighty Roman Empire, is there any reason to believe it could not happen to us?

I believe there are millions of Americans who are fed up with the moral decay of our great country. I fervently hope we will soon join together to honor God and reject sin. I believe there is still time, and I am willing to commit to God to do whatever it takes to use that time to change the moral course of this nation. Are you?

HERODIANS IN THE MEDIA

In 1952 the National Association of Broadcasters (NAB) established a review board for the television industry. The NAB screened television programs before they aired to guarantee that anti-social behavior such as illicit sexual relations and drunkenness would be filtered out and not presented as exemplary behavior in our society.

The system worked for more than a decade. In 1965, top-rated shows like "Bonanza," "The Red Skelton Hour," "I Love Lucy," "The Andy Griffith Show," and "My Three Sons" exhibited strong family values.

However, in their quest for higher ratings, the daytime serials, or soap operas, began pushing the limits of what was allowed. By the mid-1970s censorship had lost most of its power, and programs started to show increasingly graphic depictions of sex and violence. Women in skimpy clothing became a familiar sight. Unmarried couples climbing into the same bed became common. Today, those partners are likely to be same-sex couples.

The 1990s brought the Internet, which offers pornography in your home with just the click of a mouse and a credit-card number. Today, there is no longer any serious censorship in television programming or in the film industry. Most homes in America have television, cable, and satellite broadcasting anything they want, right into our homes, without *any* form of censorship whatsoever.

The movie-rating system also has become meaningless. "PG-13" means you can show your 13 year-old child some nudity, some harsh language and some violence. Film companies shy from producing G-rated movies these days because they say there simply is no longer the audience to make them financially feasible. Spurred on by an astonishing lack of moral outcry, producers are free to portray the kinds of graphic sex and violence necessary to lure a higher audience share. And the most frightening fact of all: they produce, air, and sell only what people will watch. How has the media convinced America that society wants to watch endless immorality, 24/7?

I am certain that Satan's evil forces are jubilant at the ravages this disease has wrought upon families and children. What better way to help cripple the world and prepare for Satan's takeover than to create a generation of easily influenced orphans?

(It's fair to note that there are an increasing number of family-friendly films and movies in the theaters these days that strike at the heart of urgent moral issues. But they're difficult to finance, and theaters often face pressure from secularist organizations not to screen them. A movie about notorious serial killer Kermit Gosnell, for example, had an extraordinarily difficult time being screened in 750 theaters across the country—the minimum number that Netflix will consider before it picks up a film after its theatrical run. And, though *Gosnell: The Untold Story of America's Most Prolific Serial Killer* was a powerful portrayal of the dark side of the abortion industry, very few mainstream movie critics bothered to review it. I suppose violence is only worth writing about if it happens to unborn babies.)

If you are starting to feel a creeping sensation, it's the spirit of the Herodians, leavening its way through the moral fabric of our society. When will the Church step into its God-given role and exercise her authority? It's time for Christians to stand up and say "No more!" Say it to the media when they sweep Christian morals under the rug. Not to stand against these evils is to allow them. To allow them is to approve of them. To approve of them is to join the perversion.

When will Christians draw the line between good and evil, start pushing back the powers of darkness, and root out the leaven of the Herodians from society? This is not why Jesus came. Jesus said, "The thief does not come, except to steal and kill and destroy. I came that they may have life, and that they may have it more abundantly" (John 10:10).

EXAMINE YOUR WORLD

It is time we examine the grip the world has on us. Parents, let's commit to taking close looks at the books and websites our children are viewing. Go through them thoroughly. Just because it shows a 14 year-old skateboarder on the outside doesn't mean you should trust the advertising, writing, and pictures on the inside.

Do the same with the television shows your kids watch, including cartoons, and especially the commercials between the shows. Put Internet blocks on your computer and restrictions on your wifi.

You may say, "Well, I don't want to offend little Johnny by taking away his television and Internet, Pastor!" Let me tell you, you'll offend his precious soul much more

CHAPTER 4 | THE LEAVEN OF THE HERODIANS

when you, as his parent, allow him to keep them and be influenced by them.

You may say, "But we don't want little Susie to think we lack confidence in her, so we let her have a steady boyfriend, even though we know she's probably too young. After all, everyone at her school dates." But are we lemmings, ready to follow each other off a cliff in the name of "everyone else does it? " Let me ask you this: who is more pleased when we allow these Herodian things, God or the devil?

Oh, that the Lord would help us raise young people who will think like God's children, talk like God's children, and act like God's children. We are God's chosen and anointed. Let's restrict the leaven our children can access.

ASK, AND GOD WILL CLEANSE YOU!

The leaven of the Herodians hinders our judgment. We must stop ignoring it, because it will not simply go away. The cleansing water of the Word of God must drive it out.

Illicit sex might please for a moment.

Pornographic magazines might please for a moment. Sin might gratify for a moment. But hell will last for eternity. Jesus asked his followers,

> For whoever would save his life will lose it. But whoever would lose his life for My sake and the gospel's will save it. For what does it profit a man if he gains the whole world and loses his own soul? (Mark 8:35-36).

John Lake was a missionary in Central Africa when an epidemic of bubonic plague broke out in one of the villages where he was ministering. Hundreds were dying; it was one of the most contagious outbreaks the area had ever known.

The government sent a ship with supplies and corps of doctors. Noticing that Lake didn't seem infected, one of the doctors asked him what he had found to inoculate himself against the virus that was wiping out his village. "Brother," Lake answered, "it is the law of the Spirit of life in Christ Jesus. As long as I keep my soul in contact with the living God so His Spirit is flowing into my soul and body, no germ can attach itself to me."

The doctor apparently didn't believe him, so Lake proposed he conduct a simple experiment: "Go over to one of these dead people and take the foam that comes from their lungs after death. Put it under the microscope, and you will see masses of living germs. You will find they are alive, but I can put the foam in my hand and the germs will die instantly." They did as Lake instructed, and were surprised to find it just as he said. "Why is that?" they questioned in amazement.

"That is the law of the Spirit of life in Christ Jesus," Lake answered. "My spirit and my body are so filled with the blessed presence of God, it even oozes from my pores."

The germs had come in contact with the Holy Ghost repellent—a life lived and dedicated fully to God, a life that repels the forces of darkness! It is time for the world to fear the power of God, and for us Christians to stop fearing the devil. As Paul wrote to the church at Thessalonica,

Then the lawless one will be revealed, whom the Lord will consume with the breath of His

mouth, and destroy with the brightness of His presence, even him, whose coming is in accordance with the working of Satan with all power and signs and false wonders, and with all deception of unrighteousness among those who perish, because they did not receive the love for the truth that they might be saved (2 Thessalonians 2:8-10).

Did you read that? The Word will consume the enemy! Brightness shall destroy the darkness, and the leaven of the Herodians will be no more!

COME OUT FROM AMONG THEM!

I urge you therefore, brothers, by the mercies of God, that you present your bodies as a living sacrifice, holy, and acceptable to God, which is your reasonable service of worship. Do not be conformed to this world, but be transformed by the renewing of your mind, that you may prove what is the good and acceptable and perfect will of God" (Romans 12:1-2).

Have you noticed? Christian music sounds more and more like the music of the world these days. Christian television shows are hard to tell apart from "New Age" programs. Our divorce rate matches the world's. Our rates of alcoholism and drug abuse are probably about the same. John Osteen (Joel's late father, for you younger folks) once said the world has become so churchy and the Church so worldly, that it is hard to tell the difference anymore.

Today, God is calling for a great exodus. He is calling for the Church to come out of bondage. He is calling for us to come out from among them and be separate. He is calling the Church not to touch the unclean thing. He is calling His Church to be sanctified from the world, to hate the world and all that is in it.

Jesus said,

Truly, truly I say to you, unless a grain of wheat falls into the ground and dies, it remains alone. But if it dies, it bears much fruit. He who loves his life will lose it. And he who hates his life in this world will keep it for eternal life. If anyone serves Me, he must follow Me. Where I am, there will My servant be also. If anyone serves Me, the Father will honor him (John 12:24-26).

Let's not misunderstand God's intention here. Jesus wants us to die to the power of the material possessions of the world, to come out from under that mindset; He wants us to forget about "things." It doesn't mean we should not have material possessions. God's Church and His obedient followers should have the best our loving Father has to give us—and all He has is the best!

I'm not trying to give the impression that I'm a harbinger of doom. But I've been preaching for more than four decades now, and I see fewer and fewer preachers willing to preach this message anymore. That's why the leaven of the Herodians is creeping into the Church. That's why we're constantly following up on our new "converts," trying to shepherd them back into our

CHAPTER 4 | THE LEAVEN OF THE HERODIANS

pews.

Preachers, pastors, and evangelists need to preach the need to live a life separated from the world. Just as the Jewish fathers of old went through the house, cleansing it of all leaven, so must we go through our own lives, searching our hearts, and challenging ourselves to live pure and holy before God. The apostle John wrote,

> Do not love the world or the things in the world. If anyone loves the world, the love of the Father is not in him. For all that is in the world—the lust of the flesh, the lust of the eyes, and the pride of life—is not of the Father, but is of the world. The world and its desires are passing away, but the one who does the will of God lives forever" (1 John 2:15-17).

God doesn't want us as Christians to see how close to the world we can get and still be saved. He wants us to be the kind of people who try to get as far away from the world as we can, and still be walking on the Earth.
Try this experiment: take a glass of clear water and a glass of muddy water. Pour some of the clean water into the

glass of muddy water. Did the clean water clear up the muddy water? No, it's still as muddy as ever. Now pour some muddy water into the clean water. Did the muddy water taint the clean water? Yes, visibly.

The lesson? It's far easier for a Christian to be tainted by mixing with the world than it is for a non-Christian to be cleaned by mixing with us. This doesn't mean that we stop reaching out to a lost, unsaved world; but it means that we don't join ourselves to a world covered in the muck and mire of Herodian leaven. There are only two kingdoms: the Kingdom of God and the kingdom of Satan. We cannot flirt with one while claiming the other. That is the reason why many people cannot stand "church." They have one foot in the Church and the other in the world. And a house divided will fall!

CHAPTER 5

THE LEAVEN OF THE CORINTHIANS

Webster defines the word "Corinthian" as "a merry, profligate man, completely given up to dissipation and licentiousness." The city of Corinth was known in biblical times as a town of gross immorality. It was the leading commercial city in Greece, and was the symbol of worldly luxury. It was a "happening city," the Las Vegas of its day. The leaven of the Corinthians was far worse in magnitude and frequency than even the leaven of the Herodians. One of the factors that led to the Corinthians' excessive sensuality was the Corinthian worship of Aphrodite, their goddess of love and beauty. There was even a temple dedicated solely to the worship of Aphrodite. Because of the prevalent attitude in Corinth, the members of the church there had either too cavalier a notion about God's grace or too tolerant an attitude about sexual immorality. Apparently, it was no secret that a member of the congregation had been taking his father's wife as a sexual partner!

In his first letter, Paul named the sin and took the Corinthian church to task for allowing the behavior to continue:

> *It is actually reported that there is sexual immorality among you, and such immorality as is not even named among the Gentiles, that a man has his father's wife. But you are arrogant. Instead you should have mourned, so that he who has done this deed might be removed from among you. For indeed, though absent in body but present in spirit, I have already, as if I were present, judged him who has done this deed, in the name of our Lord Jesus Christ. When you are assembled, along with my spirit, in the power of our Lord Jesus Christ, deliver him*

to Satan for the destruction of the flesh, so that the spirit may be saved on the day of the Lord Jesus (1 Corinthians 5:1-5).

Paul told them that allowing that sort of behavior was unacceptable, and he admonished the Church to expel the man:

Your boasting is not good. Do you not know that a little yeast leavens the whole batch? For what have I to do with judging those also who are outside? Do you not judge those who are inside? But God judges those who are outside. Therefore "put away from among yourselves that wicked person" (1 Corinthians 5:6, 12-13).

THE RACE OF LIFE

The leaven of immorality was ravaging the entire city of Corinth. Paul knew the only way to root out this leaven was to instruct the Corinthians to keep their bodies under subjection and to focus on the eternal rewards gained at the end of the race of life.

The Isthmian Games were held near Corinth, so the Corinthians were well acquainted with athletic contests. When Paul wrote to them, he used terminology and examples they could easily relate to:

> Do you not know that all those who run in a race run, but one receives the prize? So run, that you may obtain it. Everyone who strives for the prize exercises self-control in all things. Now they do it to obtain a corruptible crown, but we an incorruptible one. So, therefore, I run, not with uncertainty. So I fight, not as one who beats the air. But I bring and keep my body under subjection, lest when preaching to others I myself should be disqualified
>
> (1 Corinthians 9:24-27).

Paul urged the Corinthians to keep their bodies as if they were training for a grueling race. He told them to keep their fleshly desires under the same kind of subjection, restraint, and discipline it would take to win that race.

But the Corinthians lacked respect for authority and did not readily accept apostolic leadership. They wanted to be free to do their own thing. Initially, they didn't respond when Paul shared scriptural instructions for their behavior. Paul responded to their rejection of authority by reminding them that they needed godly men as their leaders—because no man could properly govern without the wisdom of God:

For the wisdom of this world is foolishness with God. For it is written, "He catches the wise in their own craftiness," and again, "The Lord knows the thoughts of the wise, that they are vain" (1 Corinthians 3:19-20).

Paul wrote to the leaders in Corinth, who in his absence had become arrogant, overbearing, and self-indulgent. The Corinthian leaders had tried to seize control of the Church. He responded to them by emphasizing the need to be a man of God, not a man of one's own understanding:

For I know nothing against myself. Yet I am not justified by this. But He who judges me is the Lord. Therefore judge nothing before the appointed time until the Lord comes. He will bring to light the hidden things of darkness and will reveal the purposes of the hearts. Then everyone will have commendation from God.

Brothers, I have figuratively applied these things to myself and to Apollos for your sakes, so that you may learn from us not to think of men above that which is written, and that not one of you would be arrogant for one against another" (1 Corinthians 4:4-6).

HE WHO SELF-GOVERNS HAS A FOOL FOR A LEADER

The undisciplined leaven of the Corinthians rejects authority. When we allow that leaven to creep into the Church, authority withers and direction is lost.

If we will learn to honor the Church authority God has placed over us, we will have less difficulty honoring the direct authority of God. When we obey the leaders He has placed over us, we expect Him to entrust us with His blessings and increasing responsibilities in His kingdom on Earth. All we have to do is to hear the voice of God through those whom God has placed over us, and respond to that voice as if God Himself were speaking to us.

It is vital that we learn and know God's Word for ourselves, so no man can lead us astray: "Beloved, do not believe every spirit, but test the spirits to see whether they are from God, because many false prophets have gone out into the world" (1 John 4:1).

We need to be on guard against a "know-it-all" attitude. We do not respect authority because that authority is right, but because it is authority. Authority can be wrong, but we must still respect it. If an authority is egregiously wrong, the Lord will deal with it according to His plan and purpose, and in His timing. Nothing goes unnoticed in His universe, and we must trust that He rights all wrongs.

When I was young, teachers were always right —period. Today, people are readily willing to give their opinion about how the pastor is wrong, the teacher is wrong, the principal is wrong. Everyone seems to have problems except the person doing the criticizing! That critical spirit is the biggest indicator of a person who refuses to submit to authority.

If we are willing to come under authority, especially as we pray for those whom the Lord put over us as our leaders, then we will experience a peaceful and productive life:

> *Therefore I exhort first of all that you make supplications, prayers, intercessions, and thanksgivings for everyone, for kings and for all who are in authority, that we may lead a quiet and peaceful life in all godliness and honesty* (1 Timothy 2:1-2).

On the other hand, when we do not honor authority, we come out from under the covering of God and we become subject to the attacks and curses of the enemy. We must gently, but firmly, rein in people who criticize and confront the leaders in authority over us. We must bring those who worry and whine into an understanding of the destructive disharmony of their spirit and how it works against the purposes of God.

Our primary responsibility is to make it to heaven, to finish the race. We are responsible for doing everything in our power to see to it that we get there. But we are not in charge of matters that are beyond our control or influence, so there's no use in worrying about them. Submit them to the Lord in prayer, and worry not. If those who have authority over you are abusing their authority, trust that God will see to it that they answer to Him for their actions. And, believe me, He will!

COUNTERING REBELLIOUS SPIRITS

So how do we deal with those who blatantly disregard authority? By showing them grace, by speaking to them in uplifting and encouraging words and by setting examples of good work.

"But Pastor," the gripers gripe, "my wife and I just can't accept your decision that we should stay together. We've talked it over and we know we need to divorce. We can still serve God as singles."

These poor souls refuse to yield to spiritual authority, which equates to lack of trust in God and lack of faith in the leaders He appoints over us. It is essential that we each find our place in the Church, to function in that place, and to bear fruit—which brings increase to the body of Christ.

Some people who come to the church offices for personal ministry aren't truly interested in hearing the truth. They're actually looking for validation. They need someone to agree with the decision they have already made on their own. If the person in authority does not agree with the decision they've made, they reject the counsel and leave the church.

It breaks my heart, but people sometimes get angry with me when they seek my counsel, because they've already made up their minds about what they are going to do. Young couples come to me for premarital counseling and announce, "We have decided to get married." If I respond, "You've made the wrong choice," they are shocked.

"What do you mean we made the wrong choice?"

they demand.

"Have you talked to any spiritual authority over you about this union?" I respond.

"No, no. God told us!" they reply with straight-faced conviction.

At that point, what else can I say? After all, I am not God, nor am I above Him. I stand and tell them, "If you say God told you, well, that zips my lips. I'm done. There's no need for my counsel."

People too often make their decisions first and then want God and His men of authority to bless their decision. Sometimes when I ask young people the question, "What do your parents think about the person you are marrying?" I hear comments like, "My parents think he is too immature," or, "My mom and dad think she is nice, but they say we should wait."

Parental counsel seems to make little difference to much of the youth of this society (and that is not unique to the current generation of young people; their parents likely had the same attitude). They have not been taught respect for authority. That rejection of authority is learned in their very own homes.

Such lack of authority is the rebellious leaven of Corinth. It's still around today. Isn't it high time to repent of this leaven and yield to the authority God has placed over us, calling on Him in prayer to guide us through their counsel?

Let's commit to teaching our children to make wise life choices based on the Word of God. If we faithfully teach our children, when they become adults they will be unified in strengthening the moral fabric of society instead of becoming part of the disintegration of the family.

Just as in Old Testament days, rooting out the leaven starts in the home. Children need to understand the chain of command in the home, with the father at the head and the mother at his side, as God has specified. Every time we step out of that chain of authority, we invite trouble that breeds rebellion and destruction.

I believe a rebellious spirit was bred in this nation in the early 1960s, a spirit that today is accepted as normal decades later. Even in our Christian school, parents are constantly coming into the office telling us their child has been issued a detention when he "did nothing wrong"—as if the school is handing out detentions for no reason. If the parents have difficulty honoring authority, then their children are not going to respect authority either.

    It is our responsibility as parents to teach respect for authority to our children. We must teach them terms such as "mister," "ma'am," and "sir." We must teach them words like "thank you" and "please" and "pardon me." We must teach them by our own example how a person in authority under God walks in the ways of the Lord. Politeness, respect, and chivalry aren't dead; the enemy of our families has only taken them captive. Let's take them back!

    In the midst of the constant violence and negatives portrayed in television and movies, let your children see their authority figures doing the things of God in their lives. Let them see you seeking God through prayer, Scripture reading, study, and service to others.

Let them experience charity, encouragement, nurturing, obedience to God's will, and a deep concern for the needs of others. Insist that the family unit reflect God's authority, starting with the relationship of the husband and the wife:

> Wives, be submissive to your own husbands as unto the Lord. For the husband is the head of the wife, just as Christ is the head and Savior of the church, which is His body. But as the church submits to Christ, so also let the wives be to their own husbands in everything.
>
> Husbands, love your wives, just as Christ also loved the church and gave Himself for it, that He might sanctify and cleanse it with the washing of water by the word, and that He might present to Himself a glorious church, not having spot, or wrinkle, or any such thing, but that it should be holy and without blemish. In this way men ought to love their wives as their own bodies. He who loves his wife loves

himself. For no one ever hated his own flesh, but nourishes and cherishes it, just as the Lord cares for the church (Ephesians 5:22-29).

Godly authority governs in godly love, nourishing and cherishing those who are governed, just as God nourishes and cherishes His Church. If husbands and wives are to live as an example of Jesus, then they will love, care for, nurture and cherish each other.

Husbands are called by God to be loving leaders, providers and protectors. Wives are called to be nurturers and cooperative partners. Both are called to esteem and respect each other: "However, let each one of you love his wife as himself, and let the wife see that she respects her husband" (Ephesians 5:33).

CORINTHIAN MALICE

The Corinthians harbored evil thoughts toward Paul, often holding malice against him. Malice is an evil thought-life, and it is part of the leaven of the Corinthians.

God commands all of us to be ready to forgive and

to radiate the love of Jesus in our relationships with others.

> *Finally, brothers, whatever things are true, whatever things are honest, whatever things are just, whatever things are pure, whatever things are lovely, whatever things are of good report, if there is any virtue, and if there is any praise, think on these things. Do those things which you have both learned and received, and heard and seen in me, and the God of peace will be with you* (Philippians 4:8-9).

God wants us to do good things for one another. He wants us to dwell on pure, holy, lovely things of good report. As we do so, there will be no room for malicious thoughts in our minds.

Finally, we need to pray and ask God to help us practice the Biblical principles He has given us to walk in, and to reflect His love in all we do and say. It is essential that we cast out the leaven of malice that permeates much of the Church today. If you will covenant with God right now, today, to live the life of God and to resist the lies and deceit of the enemy, then you will see your family flourish in love and peacefulness. And your children develop into men and women of substance and wisdom who are a living reflection of the glory of God.

The Corinthians were heavy on the gifts and light on the fruit. Everyone wants to talk in tongues,

God wants us to do good things for one another. He wants us to dwell on pure, holy, lovely things of good report. As we do so, there will be no room for malicious thoughts in our minds.

Finally, we need to pray and ask God to help us practice the Biblical principles He has given us to walk in, and to reflect His love in all we do and say. It is essential that we cast out the leaven of malice that permeates much of the Church today. If you will covenant with God right now, today, to live the life of God and to resist the lies and deceit of the enemy, then you will see your family flourish in love and peacefulness. And your children develop into men and women of substance and wisdom who are a living reflection of the glory of God.

The Corinthians were heavy on the gifts and light

on the fruit. Everyone wants to talk in tongues, prophesy, preach, work miracles, and manifest the gifts of healing. But few are willing to pay the price of living in accordance with God's mandates. If we ask Him to, God will cleanse our thought-lives and purify the motives of our hearts.

I SEE A DAY . . .

While we remain on this earth, I see a day when Christians will minister the Gospel of God as His ambassadors and servants. Our hands will minister to a hurting and dying world that desperately needs our blessed Savior.

I see a day when we will reflect and radiate the bright light of a Church totally transformed by God's love —a light that will attract the world to our door, begging us to teach them the hope God has shown us through Jesus Christ.

I see a day when the world will see the distinction between the muck and mud of the Corinthians and the glory and grace of the redeemed.

I see a day when the leaven of the Corinthians—gross immorality, malice, backbiting, and lack of respect for authority—will be as repugnant to us as they are to God.

I see a day when those in the world will come to us, desperately seeking to find the things they have never experienced, anxious to be what we are: reflections of the Christ Who dwells within us!

I see a day when we will be a cleansed Church, a bride ready for the bridegroom, purified by God's transforming grace.

I see a day coming when the world will look at Christians and cry, "I want what they have! I want to be like they are. They love each other so deeply. They serve each other so willingly. I want to experience that kind of relationship, that kind of joy in my life!"

CHAPTER 6

THE LEAVEN OF THE GALATIANS

The leaven of the Galatians is the human (and futile) attempt to justify our worthiness to Christ through the works of the flesh.

The congregation of the Church at Galatia was a mixture of Gentiles and converted Jews. Many converts from Judaism still scrupulously kept the ceremonies and other obligations of the Mosaic Law. They insisted on legalistic requirement—such as circumcision—as necessary components of salvation, even after the apostles and other elders in Jerusalem had dealt with those matters. They attempted to justify their relationship with God by the works of their flesh and to establish their own righteousness through the Law instead of through "righteousness due to faith," which was provided by the New Covenant.

Paul accused these "false brethren" of stirring up division solely for the purpose of keeping true converts in bondage to the old law and thereby under the control of those who were causing the dissension:

> *This happened because false brothers were secretly brought in, who sneaked in to spy out our liberty, which we have in Christ Jesus, that they might bring us into bondage. Yet we know that a man is not justified by the works of the law, but through faith in Jesus Christ. Even we have believed in Christ Jesus, so that we might be justified by faith in Christ, rather than by the works of the law. For by the works of the law no flesh shall be justified*
> (Galatians 2:4, 16).

Like the Sadducees and the Pharisees, the Galatians opposed Paul, and even tried to discredit him as an apostle. They felt that by mixing in old Jewish tradition and laws with the New Covenant, such as requiring new Christians to be circumcised, they would pacify the Jews and keep them from opposing their congregation so violently. Paul exposed their motives by telling them that what they were actually trying to do was to avoid suffering persecution for Christ: "It is those who desire to make a good showing in the flesh that try to compel you to be circumcised, only that they may not be persecuted for the cross of Christ" (Galatians 6:12).

However, the Galatians argued that circumcision would profit the church at Galatia and advance them in Christianity by making them true sons of Abraham, to whom the covenant of circumcision was originally given. Paul thoroughly refuted the contentions of these false Christians and built up the Galatian brothers so they would stand firm in Christ:

> *Christ has redeemed us from the curse of the law by being made a curse for us—as it is written, "Cursed is everyone who hangs on a tree"—so that the blessing of Abraham might come on the Gentiles through Jesus Christ, that we might receive the promise of the Spirit through faith* (Galatians 3:13-14).

Paul's direct and powerful message stated that anyone who chooses to follow the law, rather than live under God's grace through faith in Christ, is bound to follow it in its entirety. It's impossible for men to follow the law, and that is one of the reasons Christ came to save us:

> *For freedom Christ freed us. Stand fast therefore and do not be entangled again with the yoke of bondage. Indeed I, Paul, say to you that if you become circumcised, Christ will profit you nothing. I testify again to every man who is circumcised that he is obligated to keep the whole law. You have been cut off from Christ, whoever of you are justified by law; you have fallen from grace* (Galatians 5:1-4).

There are major denominations today whose teaching is rife with this same false leaven as that of the Galatians.

JUST ONE MORE DEED

"For by grace you have been saved through faith,

and this is not of yourselves. It is the gift of God, not of works, so that no one should boast" (Ephesians 2:8-9).

"I'm going to heaven because I never fail to go to church on Sunday, I sing in the choir, and I help serve hotdogs at all the church outreach events."

"Lord, you have written my name in the Book of Life because I say the rosary every single day—sometimes twice."

"Father, I am saved because I work with the homeless people down at the food center every Wednesday afternoon."

"Jesus, you love me because I visit the sick at the nursing home and bring them flowers every Sunday afternoon."

Do those sentiments sound familiar? Of course they do. But goodness is not godliness, and good works do not save—they never have and they never will.

Whatever we do out of a routine that does not flow spontaneously from our hearts toward God is religion and is the work of the flesh. Anything can become dead, lifeless, and religious when it separates us from a true relationship with God.

I use the word "religious" to describe anything that becomes repetitious and mechanical in our worship, devoid of the freshness of the Spirit of God. Anything done out of routine, and not out of a heart hungry for God, is a work of the flesh. Many good things can become religious:

- Shouting His praises can become religious.
- Loud singing, clapping, and dancing can become religious.
- Quiet, soft songs can become religious.
- Jumping up and down can become religious.
- Standing solemnly can become religious.
- Folding our hands and bowing our head to pray can become religious.
- Kneeling down to pray can become religious.

Paul told the Galatians, "You started off in the spirit, but then entered into a 'works' dogma. You cannot earn your way to heaven."

The good news for you and for me is that we don't

need to labor under "works" any longer. God loved us so much that He gave us Himself, and that's all the work that needs to be done!

If you believe in the Lord Jesus Christ with all your heart, mind, soul, and strength, and if you confess with your mouth that Jesus Christ of Nazareth came down from heaven, died on a cross, and shed His blood for your sins, then you are going to heaven. There are no "works" involved in that. He rose again from the dead for your justification, went back to the Father and sent down the Holy Ghost, who fills your life.

God did all of that; we did none of it. All we need to do is believe that Jesus is returning again to receive us, because we accepted the price paid for our sins when He shed His redeeming, forgiving, life-giving blood.

Does that mean when we love God, we don't have to do anything? No. It means that you will want to do for Him, out of the love you have for Him in your heart—not out of obligation or dedication to a works-based faith. When our heart is filled with love for Him, the outward actions of that love will naturally flow, because love is a verb that expresses itself in actions.

When Christians first begin to walk with the Lord, they are excited and exuberant. But many gradually slip into a works mentality that allows the devil's condemnation to enter, mostly because they begin to realize there is no way they can ever work hard enough or long enough to "justify" their eternal salvation. The solution to this deception is that we must cast out all dependence on good works as our qualification for acceptance by God.

He has a much better plan for us. It's called grace, and it is a free gift from our loving Lord! As Paul wrote to the churches at Rome,

> *For all have sinned and come short of the glory of God, being justified freely by His grace through the redemption that is in Christ Jesus, whom God has set forth to be a propitiation through faith, in His blood, for a demonstration of His righteousness, because in His forbearance God had passed over the sins previously committed, to prove His*

righteousness at this present time so that He might be just and be the justifier of him who has faith in Jesus (Romans 3:23-26).

THE NATURE OF GRACE

Here's an acrostic to help you remember key facts about grace:

G stands for gift, the principle of grace.

R stands for redemption, the purpose of grace.

A stands for access, the privilege of grace.

C stands for character, the product of grace.

E stands for eternal life, the prospect of grace.

Grace is the free gift of God. There is nothing we can do to earn it. What an incredible gift it is!

If there is nothing we can do to earn it, then there also is nothing we can do to keep it. And if there is nothing we can do to earn it or keep it, then we can't do anything that would cause us to lose it. When we sin Jesus Christ advocates for us before the Father, pleading our case.

We do not receive grace by joining someone's church. We do not receive grace by sitting on the front pew. No one has any more or less grace than anyone else. God loved us in the depth of our sin. If He loved us then, He can surely love us now.

Make a promise to remind yourself: "He loves me!" Say it often, because that simple reminder is the greatest defense against the onslaught of hell. It's the greatest defense against the lie that tells us, "You are not doing enough for God. How could He love someone like you? You don't have salvation!" Those are lies!

Say it to yourself, "God loves me." Period. End of story. *His grace is free.*

Redemption is the purpose of grace. To "redeem" means to return to the original state of affairs. In the mind and heart of God, every human being drawing breath on this planet is forgiven. Even the person in the deepest depth of sin is forgiven. All we have to do is ask God for it, and then accept it.

You may ask "What about Hitler?" or someone else known for their viciousness and sinful acts. Let me tell you, if Adolph Hitler would have knelt down, cried out to God and asked for forgiveness, he would have received it. Even though he had instigated and overseen the death of millions of Jews, God would have forgiven Hitler. That's because God's grace is unlimited, without measure!

"What about one of the most notorious anti-Christian terrorists of the early first century, a man who went after Christians to seek their imprisonment and death, a man who stood by as an accomplice when his co-conspirators gruesomely stoned one of the disciples to death?"

Yes, even Saul was forgiven when he repented and asked for forgiveness. He went on to become the great Apostle Paul. So many people believe the lie that they cannot be forgiven. When was the last time you murdered one of Christ's appointed own? If Paul could be forgiven, anyone can.

Jesus says, "It is finished. Forgiveness is yours. If you had an abortion, you can be forgiven. If you are on your fourth marriage, you can be forgiven. If you abused—or aborted—your child, you can be forgiven. No matter what crime, no matter what offense you have committed, My love is greater than your offense, and you can be forgiven if you will repent and receive Me as the propitiation for your sins."

When Jesus rose from the dead, His resurrection meant we were justified. Jesus justifies us, not our works! If there had been any sin that was capable of separating us from the love of God, Jesus would still be in that tomb today, paying the price. If Jesus had not shed His blood to forgive the sins we are entangled in right now, if God the Father had not forgiven us for every sin we have ever committed up to this very moment, Christ would still be in that tomb.

But on the third day, He arose from the dead, victorious over death, hell, and the grave, and the Father said, "Enough! That is enough. The price is now paid for every human being that will ever draw a breath of air on this earth! I have forgiveness enough for every single one, and it flows through My freely-given grace."

Gypsy Smith tells the story of an atheist who placed an ad in the local newspaper proclaiming that on a particular Sunday he was going to stand out in a field, curse the name of God and damn Him. If there was a God, this atheist reasoned, fire would come spewing out of heaven.

At 2 p.m., the atheist went out to the field and started yelling and screaming at God, swearing every oath he could swear. He cursed at the heavens until he was red in the face, and blue veins were popping out of his neck. Finally, in exasperation, he told the crowd, "See, I told you there was no God."

An old lady waved her hanky and said, "Excuse me, sir. All you have proven today is that God is who He says He is. He is the giver of all grace, and His grace has been extended to you today. His grace is inexhaustible, and you are still alive, proving it."

You cannot get away from it. His grace will wake you up in the middle of the night saying, "Let me in, please let me in."Jesus says to you and to me, "Listen! I stand at the door and knock. If anyone hears My voice and opens the door, I will come in and dine with him, and he with Me" (Revelation 3:20).

That is grace. He will come in! We don't have to look for Him. He is looking for us!

Redemption is the purpose of grace, to return us to the original state of affairs. His grace washes our blackened hearts so clean we are purified, like Adam and Eve in the Garden of Eden.

Access is the privilege of grace. "For through Him we both have access by one Spirit to the Father" (Ephesians 2:18). Through Calvary's bleeding Lamb, we can get from where we were, through the veil that was torn in two in the Holy of Holies, to the very throne room of God. It is there we find grace enough to help us in time of need, and it is there we can cry out "Abba, Father!"

Just imagine: God the Creator of the universe gives us free access into His very own presence! We do not need to come into a building where a security guard standing behind a podium can give us access to the presence of our Holy God. We do not need to attract the attention of a famous television preacher to give us access to God.

The veil that hung in the temple, four inches thick,

woven without seam 20 feet wide and 40 feet high, was torn from top to bottom by God, and He said, "I am coming out and you are coming in."

Run to God! Never shy away. Never hide your face in shame. Never shrink back! He has torn the veil and by His grace we have access to Him. What a privilege!

Character is the product of grace. Grace is a godly characteristic, and only the God-life flowing through us can cause it to manifest in our character. Grace is of God. When it does manifest, it is only thanks to God. The people who love me when I am unlovable are operating in something beyond themselves. They are loving me in the character of God's grace.

Grace humbles us before God. Grace is the greatest character-building stone known in the arsenal of God, for grace humbles us. That God would give us access into His presence should be a humbling wakeup call. The only reason we are allowed into the throne room of God is because—though we did not deserve it—Jesus paid our ransom and let us come into the heavenly banquet! "For the law was given through Moses; grace and truth came through Jesus Christ" (John 1:17).

Eternal life is the prospect of grace.

Just think of it: we are going to live forever! Why? Because the end product of the grace of God is eternal life.

We are alive, never to die, because inside us is immortality. We are going to live forever in the pavilions of God, walking on streets of gold, hearing angelic songs and marching and dancing to the song of the redeemed. That gives us relationship with our Creator—not just religion.

Eternal life! We have something to look forward to. Grace is not finished yet. We are going to a city whose Builder and Maker is God, and there we will be kings and priests! "Blessed and holy is he who takes part in the first resurrection. Over these the second death has no power, but they shall be priests of God and of Christ and shall reign with Him a thousand years" (Revelation 20:6).

When we get to heaven, it will not matter what we were on Earth—the President of the United States, the Queen of England, or a used-car salesman! It doesn't matter! We are all going to live on Hallelujah Avenue and Glory Boulevard! We are all going to walk on streets made of gold and live in a mansion He prepared just for us.

THE PROSPECT OF GRACE

Let me tell you what grace is going to do for me. Grace is going to a lonely hillside in eastern Kentucky. Up on that little hillside is a grave marked with the name of my uncle, who served his country in the rice paddies of Vietnam and went to be with the Lord at the age of 20. He went to war with the face of an angel and came back with half of that face gone. But I am on a journey, and one day I will see his perfect face!

I believe the prospect of grace is that one day in thet "great gettin' up morning" graves will open. The dead in Christ are going to rise first, and then we who are alive and remain shall be sent up into the clouds to be with the Lord forever! It may happen tomorrow at 2:15 p.m., or it may happen early in the morning one day next week. I don't know when it is going to happen, but I do know this: it is going to happen. What a prospect!

I am going to see loved ones who have gone on before me, and I will walk past David's restored tabernacle of praise and worship. I will pass by trees planted on either side of the River of Life, from which spring the 12 manners of fruit!

I will have the privilege of climbing up before the Great White Throne of Almighty God, and bowing down before Him. I will behold the One with the nail prints in His hands and in His feet—the One with the open side from which came blood and water, the One Who saved a sinner like me: "Then he showed me a pure river of the water of life, clear as crystal, flowing from the throne of God and of the Lamb. . . . They shall see His face, and His name shall be on their foreheads" (Revelation 22:1, 4). That is the prospect of grace—eternal life, to live forever with God!

THE PRICE OF SALVATION

Come with me to the scene of the crucifixion. They plait a crown of thorns and pierce it into His brow. The Roman's whip gouges chunks of flesh from His back;

CHAPTER 6 | THE LEAVEN OF THE GALATIANS

it hangs in bloody strips from His bones. They kick and prod Him through the cobblestone streets of Jerusalem, mocking Him, spitting on Him, striking Him over and over.

On the cross, He cries, "I thirst," and they give Him vinegar to drink. His muscles tremble under the weight of our sin. Blood streams down His forehead to His brow. He drops His head forward and blood falls to the ground, splashing in the dusty soil of Calvary.

Hear Him say, "This, My blood, is for you."

He paid the full price, and mankind was free.

How blessed we are! Our salvation is not dependent on the length of our skirts, or whether we have stripes on our shirts, zippers or buttons on our jackets.

Through grace, we can be different. We do not have to be bound up as children of God, forced into molds where we must look like everyone else.

The leaven of Galatia leavens the whole lump. It makes the whole thing the same. God said He was not going to build His church out of leaven. He is not going to build it out of bricks that all looked the same, bricks that came from the same mold. He is going to build His house with living stones, and He is the Stonecutter. He is the One who is going to shape us, mold us, and make us: as Peter wrote,

> *Coming to Him as to a living stone who is rejected by men, but chosen by God and precious, you also, as living stones, are being built up into a spiritual house as a holy priesthood to offer up spiritual sacrifices that are acceptable to God through Jesus Christ* (1 Peter 2:4-5).

If we would simply tell people the truth about how they can get to God, they will be so hungry to live for God they will naturally shun wrong and do right! If we will faithfully hold up the standard of the cross for the world, people will turn from evil and run to righteousness! So let's tell the truth, and be faithful.

THE LEGALISM LIE

Salvation is by grace—and grace alone. It is given

through nothing less and nothing more than the blood of Jesus Christ. We don't get saved by following some prescribed code or by doing a certain set of things. That is legalism—a trap the Jewish leaders of Jesus' time had fallen into and were taking to the extreme, controlling people's lives through impossible rules and regulations, none of which they themselves followed: "They fasten heavy loads that are hard to carry and lay them on men's shoulders, but they themselves will not move them with their finger" (Matthew 23:4).

    Charles Finney, when asked by one of his professors what he was going to do after law school, replied, "Put out a shingle and practice law."

    The professor said, "Then what?"

    "Get rich," was Finney's reply.

    "Then what?"

    "Retire."

    "Then what?"

    "Die."

    Moving his chair up to his desk and pulling his glasses from his eyes, that elderly squire then asked the riveting question, "Then what?"

All Finney could say at that point was, "The judgment."

Then he clasped his head in his hands and ran out and found a place by a stump in the woods and wept his way to salvation. Finney experienced the saving blood of Christ in the privacy of the woods, and he let that blood change his life.

Like Finney, so many Christians first experience God in their hearts. Then, at some point in their walk with Him, they fall into the trap of legalism—trying to do works to "earn" salvation.

COVENANT SIGN

For freedom Christ freed us. Stand fast therefore and do not be entangled again with the yoke of bondage. Indeed I, Paul, say to you that if you become circumcised, Christ will profit you nothing (Galatians 5:1-2).

The Bible talks about circumcision because it is a

sign of the Covenant. God instructed all the sons of Israel to be circumcised as a sign of covenant relationship. Circumcision represents the cutting of flesh and the spilling of blood under the Old Covenant. Before Jesus died on Calvary, this act was what gave Jews their right standing with God.

God never breaks His covenant. He never alters His covenant.

Some people wonder why the Jewish people seem to be able to show up in any country of the world with nothing more than the will to survive, and within a few years are living in the finest homes in the city.

When a Jewish boy is circumcised on the eighth day after his birth, the Jews believe that child is entering into covenant with God. So, does circumcision, itself, save them? Of course not. However, God did promise Abraham:

> *I will indeed bless you and I will indeed multiply your descendants as the stars of the heavens and as the sand that is on the seashore. Your descendants will possess the gate of their*

enemies. Through your offspring all the nations of the earth will be blessed, because you have obeyed My voice (Genesis 22:17-18).

Just think a moment about that little expanse of land named "Israel." Jesus called the city of Jerusalem the City of Peace. Yet no other place in the world has been more fought over and has had more blood shed on it than that little strip of land on the coast of the Mediterranean Sea. It doesn't matter what Israel's enemies or adversaries do to them. Whoever curses Israel is cursed, and whoever blesses them is blessed—to this day! Scores of different groups of peoples have come and gone and the Israelites remain! God is in a covenant with the Jews, and nobody can alter that covenant: "I will bless them who bless you and curse him who curses you, and in you all families of the earth will be blessed" (Genesis 12:3).

A NEW COVENANT

The Christian congregation at Galatia was composed of many Jews who had been raised and taught in the tradition and heritage of the Abrahamic Covenant. Now they were learning something new, and they weren't finding it easy.

The New Covenant says the Messiah has already been crucified. He has already shed His blood. He has already been raised from the dead. He has already ascended back to the Father. He has already sent the Holy Spirit to the earth. But these confused Jewish Galatian brethren were still walking around Galatia trying to justify favor with God by saying things like, "I have favor with God because I am circumcised. You Gentiles are not circumcised; therefore Jehovah will have nothing to do with you."

But Paul came in and said, "Whoa! Hold on a minute! This salvation thing is not by religious works and ceremonialism! Those mean nothing to God. If you're going to try to find favor with God by being circumcised, then you must also obey every other Jewish law or perish! Christ's sacrifice is useless to you if you're counting on clearing your debt to God by keeping laws. Works in your own power disqualify you from God's grace."

Paul told the Galatians about grace. He told them that God comes to blacks, whites, yellows, and browns. He told them God loves the curly-haired ones, the straight-haired ones and the bald ones. He told them God's grace comes out of His love and from the sacrifice Jesus made for us on the cross at Calvary. He told them that salvation is a free gift that cannot be worked for: "O foolish Galatians! Who has bewitched you that you should not obey the truth? Before your eyes Jesus Christ was clearly portrayed among you as crucified?" (Galatians 3:1). In the above Scripture, Paul tells the Galatians in effect, "Listen, you started off well. Who brought on all this confusion?

Who bewitched you? Who hindered you? Who did you listen to that led you away from the elementary principle of the grace of God?"

Paul knew God was not impressed with long prayers, offerings in church, or how many church services we attend. Does that mean we should not pray? No. Does that mean we should not attend church? No. Does that mean we should not give offerings? No.

CHAPTER 6 | THE LEAVEN OF THE GALATIANS

What grace does mean is that if we think we gain favor with God as a result of our own actions, then we are as confused and deceived as those who say, "You have to be circumcised," or those who say, "We have to carry candles," or those who say, "We cannot wear jewelry or make-up."

Life in the Lord is not about works! We must get that truth deep in our spirit, so the depth of our understanding of God will increase. Otherwise, if we are not careful, we will slip into the doctrine of works, and we'll feel perpetually guilty because we can never do enough to merit God's love, and we will end up feeling condemned because we have not fulfilled our works! The devil beats Christians over the head with that rolling pin all the time, but it is in our power to stop believing his lie. When you sense the crooked finger of Lucifer beckoning you into that dark corner, shout him down in the name of Jesus that, "By GRACE I am saved, and not by works, lest anyone should boast!"

I once told the devil, "Here is my Bible, devil. I am saved by the grace of God, and I am not going to be reading this evening. Good night."

Why did I say that? Because the devil had been telling me that if I failed to read another chapter that night, I was not truly saved! So I told him, "Devil, I am not even going to read the one I was just going to read—to prove that God loves me regardless. Good night."

One of the most freeing revelations that ever came to my mind was when God spoke in my spirit several years ago and said, "Do not ever try to please me again. I am already pleased."

I responded, "Lord, what do you mean?"

"See what I see," He told me.

I said, "Lord, I cannot see it."

He repeated, "See what I see."

"I cannot see it," I said again.

He said it one more time: "See what I see."

And suddenly I saw the base of a bloody cross, and God said, "I am pleased."

Do not try to please God. He is far bigger than our ability to please Him. All you need to do is believe in the finished work of Calvary.

A BRIDGE CALLED GRACE

When we deny the fullness of God's grace, we limit His presence in our lives.

God's plan of redemption was to return us to the original state of affairs He created in the Garden of Eden. In Genesis 1 and 2 we learn that God created man in His image, after His likeness. He formed man of the dust of the ground and breathed into his nostrils the breath of life. Adam's eyes opened and God told him, "See all this, son? You're in charge of it."

We aren't told precisely how long it was before Adam's fall into sin, but it was near the very beginning, after Eve was created and before she and Adam had any children. From then until now, mankind has been involved in the dance of one step ahead and three steps back.

But with the arrival, death, and resurrection of Jesus the Messiah, the restoration of God's redemptive power into our lives returns us once again to the power to walk on this planet with authority. Why—because of who we are? No! Because God laid down a bridge, and when we walk across that bridge, He changes us into who we are now. It's called grace. God designed it before He ever created us:

> *Therefore remember that formerly you, the Gentiles in the flesh, who are called the 'uncircumcision' by the so-called 'circumcision' in the flesh by human hands, were at that time apart from Christ, alienated from the citizenship of Israel and strangers to the covenants of promise, without hope and without God in the world. But now in Christ Jesus you who were formerly far away have been brought near by the blood of Christ* (Ephesians 2:11-13).

We who were once alienated from God, separated from Him by sin, contrary to God's ways, are now able to walk with acceptance and favor on this planet in the eyes of God. With grace we can boldly approach the very throne of God and receive what He has for us. The wall between us and God, erected through sin, has been crushed by the cross of Christ on Calvary's hill, and we now have access to His very presence!

Nothing will destroy the leaven of Galatia quicker than the Church's understanding of the nature and the power of the free gift of God's grace. It is only the devil who says to you: "You cannot go to God! You haven't prayed enough! You haven't read your Bible enough. You haven't witnessed enough. You haven't done enough." But who will soon be kicking the devil in the teeth, according to God? We will! Take a look: "The God of peace will soon crush Satan under your feet" (Romans 16:20a).

Amen!

CHAPTER 7

THE CLEANSING SOLUTION

When Rip Van Winkle went to Sleepy Hollow for his incredibly long nap, King George III was ruling England and Britain reigned over the American colonies. When Rip left for his nap he saw, hanging in a shop window, an image of King George III's head.

Then, Rip slept for many years. When he awoke and came down from Sleepy Hollow, the image of King George III had been replaced with the image of another George – George Washington. Rip Van Winkle had slept through an entire revolution!

Today, much of the Church is about to sleep through another revolution: a Holy Ghost revival that is going to sweep across the land and cover the earth like ocean waters! The tidal wave of God's power and glory is about to flood the world!

The kingdom of darkness is about to be overthrown. The kingdom of light is dispelling the darkness. We are living in the end times.

It is time for the Church to do what the Church has been called of God to do: preach the Gospel to the entire world! Are you going to sleep through it?

If Adam and Eve had acted according to God's instructions, there would have been no need for a New Covenant. But mankind sinned, creating the need for a Redeemer. If Jesus had not gone to Calvary, we would still be sick, depressed, lonely, discouraged, in despair, and without hope. But Jesus shed His blood on a hillside called Golgotha. And He did it for you and for me!

Most Christians don't realize it, but the Old Covenant gave the saints far more power than we think. Much was accomplished under the Old Covenant:

And what more shall I say? For time would fail me to tell of Gideon, Barak, Samson, Jephthah, of David and Samuel and the prophets, who through faith subdued kingdoms, administered justice, obtained promises, stopped the mouths of lions, quenched the violence of fire, escaped the edge of the sword, out of weakness were made strong, became valiant in fighting, and turned the armies of foreign enemies to flight. Women received their dead raised to life again. Others were tortured and did not accept deliverance, so that they might obtain a better resurrection (Hebrews 11:32-35).

The Old Covenant saints witnessed mighty miracles at the hand of God. But man's sinful nature limited the Old Covenant. Finally God said, "It is not enough; I will make a new covenant." Yet today, under the New—and more powerful—Covenant, we think it is a miracle if a fever leaves one of our children!

WHAT'S BEHIND DOESN'T MATTER!

Under the Old Covenant, there was a great man named Jephthah, a Gileadite:

Now Jephthah the Gileadite was a mighty man of valor, but he was the son of a prostitute.

Gilead was the father of Jephthah. Gilead's wife also bore him sons. His wife's sons grew up and drove Jephthah away. They said to him, "You will not inherit anything from our father's house because you are the son of another woman" (Judges 11:1-2).

Jephthah was aware that being born of a prostitute was no fault of his; he was not ashamed. However, when his half brothers used it as an excuse to kick him out of his house and deny his inheritance, Jephthah had no choice but to go. He went to Tob, where a band of men gathered around him and served him as their commander. There, he grew in valor and military prowess.

There is no "wrong side of the tracks" when we serve God. There is no wrong lineage in Him. God created all men equal in His sight. We may be in the homeless shelter today, but we do not have to be there when the sun pops over the horizon tomorrow!

In the Bible, we have a book of instructions for understanding God's nature and to how to have a personal relationship with Him through Jesus Christ. The Bible teaches us how to live; it is our owner's manual for life. So there are no excuses for not cultivating a relationship with God.

"But I'm the wrong color."

Jesus was born in the Middle East. What color do you think He was? I bet He didn't look Swedish.

"Well, I do not speak the right language."

Then learn the new language—the Holy Ghost language!

"Well, you don't understand what kind of environment I came from."

I do understand this: 65 percent of all children of color in this nation are being raised in single-parent homes, and much of society wants them to believe they cannot amount to much.

If the Church is to free itself of leaven, then each of us must get the nonsense out of our minds that we are the wrong color, wrong size or wrong shape, or that we have the wrong nationality or the wrong education. We also must stop putting those misguided thoughts into the minds of others: "What then shall we say to these things? If God is for us, who can be against us?" (Romans 8:31).

When the children of Ammon gathered themselves to make war against Israel, the Israelites realized that they needed an experienced military leader. Who had built a reputation as the best in the land? "They said to Jephthah, 'Come and be our leader so that we may fight the Ammonites'" (Judges 11:6).

The elders of Gilead went to talk Jephthah into coming out of the land of Tob and becoming their leader. In addition to being a capable military commander, Jephthah was also wise. When the Israelites came to him with their proposal, Jephthah said, "I will lead our people in battle and fight this war—but only if you agree that if the Lord gives me victory, you will make me head over all the inhabitants of Gilead."

Israel agreed to Jephthah's terms, and he gathered mighty men from each of the tribes of Israel. Only Ephraim did not join with Jephthah. Without the forces of Ephraim, the great general Jephthah realized

CHAPTER 7 | THE CLEANSING SOLUTION

that the war could be out of balance, with him outnumbered and out armed. He knew that unless something supernatural happened immediately, he might lose the battle, and his life. The armies of Israel would perish, and he would go down in history as a failure.

Maybe it was because Jephthah was born on the wrong side of the tracks. Maybe it was because he was the son of a harlot. Maybe it was because his family had thrown him out. Maybe it was because from those difficulties he had learned not to be a quitter but rather a fighter, a warrior, a mighty man of valor.

In the midst of potential defeat, something on the inside of Jephthah rose up, and he said, "Wait a minute. I am Jephthah. I am not going to die on the battlefield! My epitaph is not going to read, 'Jephthah, man of failure!'" Like Jephthah, we too are a people of destiny. If your circumstances tell you that you are outnumbered and on the ropes, then stop listening to the negative voices of the world around you. Don't listen to those who would hold you down and keep you back and suggest that you cannot become the person God intended you to be. They are serving you leavened bread. Don't eat what they're dishing out!

A preacher friend of mine once said, "When we are full of the Word and full of the Holy Ghost, it makes us feel like we are somebody when we know we ain't nobody."

PRAY WITH URGENT FAITH

"And I tell you, ask, and it will be given to you; seek, and you will find; knock, and it will be opened to you. For everyone who asks receives, and he who seeks finds, and to him who knocks it will be opened" (Luke 11:9-10).

So what did Jephthah do? He sought God in prayer: *Jephthah made a vow to the LORD, "If You will indeed give the Ammonites into my hands, then whatever comes out from the door of my house to meet me, when I return safely from the Ammonites, will surely be the LORD's, and I will offer it up as a burnt offering"* (Judges 11:30-31).

CHAPTER 7 | THE CLEANSING SOLUTION

Do you sense, like I do, that seeking God in prayer is becoming a lost art in the body of Christ? Too many pastors are teaching less and less about prayer. When will they learn that we cannot keep leaven out of our lives without the protection of prayer?

Incredibly, the notion that prayer is passé is polluting our seminaries. A so-called "scholar" of the Harvard Divinity School once made the statement, "I do not believe that the religion of tomorrow will have any more need of petition [prayer] than it will have for any other form of magic."

I may not have all the degrees that this studied man possesses, but I do know how to read! And my Bible says,

> *If My people, who are called by My name, will humble themselves and pray, and seek My face and turn from their wicked ways, then I will hear from heaven, and will forgive their sin and will heal their land* (2 Chronicles 7:14).

Hasn't the time finally arrived for us to stop hanging around with the devil's deadbeats? Are you willing to make a covenant with God to stop mixing with people who denigrate the power of prayer and start hanging out with God's Holy Ghost prayer warriors, who know His Word is true, who know what He says is right, and who know He will bring to pass everything He promises?

You must also have faith in your prayers to God—that they will be heard and answered by a God who is eager to hear from you. Notice, I said "faith in your prayers to God," not faith in your denomination, your local church, or a Harvard Divinity School graduate. Have faith in the power of prayer to a hearing God! The old hymn writer said:

> *Sweet hour of prayer, sweet hour of prayer*
> *that calls me from a world of care,*
> *and bids me at my Father's throne*
> *make all my wants and wishes known.*
> *In seasons of distress and grief,*
> *my soul has often found relief,*
> *and oft escaped the tempter's snare*
> *by thy return, sweet hour of prayer.*

Jephthah said, "I know what I will do. I will pray!" He didn't have much time. The Ammonite and Moabite hordes were coming over the hill. Their swords glistened in the noonday sun at their imminent approach. He could hear their screaming war cries like dogs hungry to lap up Gileadite blood on the field of battle. This was no time to run a trial prayer up the flagpole and see who saluted. No time to zip over to the book store and get a book on how to pray!

When it came time to pray, did Jephthah run home and slip into his $1,000 Armani suit and ostrich boots? No! Did he go and outfit his wife in a Gucci designer dress, put bonnets on the kids' heads and say, "Okay, it's now 9:30 a.m. Gotta make sure we get to church by 10 and get praying." No! I do not find it recorded anywhere that Jephthah so much as bowed down, tilted his head over, and folded his hands like an old diver getting ready to plunge into the depths.

Jephthah merely stood on the battlefield, his life at stake, unable to wait indefinitely for God to answer this prayer, needing to quickly touch the heart of God with words that would move His hand and bring relief, and he prayed!

HOLD ON!

There is a woman in my congregation with Jephthah's same powerful determination. For 12 lonely years this woman suffered the anguish of separation from her husband. He had spent everything he earned to buy drugs to feed a habit that cost several hundred dollars a day. The man soon left his home and family, and he was gone for 12 years.

Week after week his precious wife stood in the middle of our church and declared, "I believe I received when I prayed. My husband's coming home. I am not bowing my knee to the spirit of divorce. God can do all things. With man it is impossible, but with God all things are possible to him that believe. I am not letting go. I am holding on!"

Her friends advised her, "Give it up. He's a drug addict! He has left home for good."

"I cannot help it," she replied. "I believe that I

received when I prayed. I have already set my prayer in motion, and God has already heard my prayer."

The answer to that woman's prayer did not happen that afternoon or that week. It did not happen the first year, or the fifth year, or the first decade. It was 12 long, hope-filled years later.

Was it worth the wait? Yes, absolutely! Every time I see them together, they're holding hands! When her husband finally yielded his life to the will of God, God put their lives and family back together.

That's what happens when we get the leaven out. We do not have to bow our knee to the spirit of divorce. God is powerful enough to keep a home together. Just have faith in His ability to do anything! He's the same God who parted the Red Sea. Don't you think He can hold your home together?

What God does for others, He'll do for you. Why? Because He is no respecter of persons. So don't you quit, Christian, for with God all things are possible!

PRAYING AND GIVING

Prayer moves mountains. It makes the low places high and brings the high places low. Prayer makes the crooked ways straight, and gives us hope when there is none. Prayer brings God on the scene.

Hannah, another Old Testament figure, needed to reach God with her petition for a child, when she was barren. Hannah prayed and vowed to give the child to the Lord if He would hear her cry:

So she made a vow and said, "O LORD of Hosts, if You will indeed look on the affliction of Your maidservant, and remember me and not forget Your maidservant, but will give to Your maidservant a baby boy, then I will give him to the LORD all the days of his life, and no razor shall touch his head" (1 Samuel 1:11).

Many people probably laughed and told Hannah that her prayer to have a child was dumb. They probably told her God would never answer a prayer like that. But when Hannah prayed, it touched the heart of God. The answer invaded her body, and opened her once-barren womb: "And it came to pass that Hannah conceived and bore a son. And she called his name Samuel saying, 'Because I have asked him of the LORD'" (1 Samuel 1:20). God answered her prayers so abundantly that Hannah bore Samuel, who became one of the greatest prophets of all time and numbered right up there with Moses (see Jeremiah 15:1). And God didn't stop at one child; He gave Hannah many more: "The LORD visited Hannah, so that she conceived and bore three sons and two daughters" (1 Samuel 2:21a).

And so here is Jephthah, in the heat of battle, raising up his voice with the same intensity as Hannah:

> Jephthah made a vow to the LORD, "If You will indeed give the Ammonites into my hands, then whatever comes out from the door of my house to meet me, when I return safely from the Ammonites, will surely be the LORD's, and I will offer it up as a burnt offering"
> (Judges 11:30-31).

Jephthah vowed his daughter to virginity in service to the Lord, the way Hannah did with her son Samuel.

Jephthah said, "God, if you will deliver this enemy into my hands, if you will deliver the children of Ammon into my hand, and I return home in peace, then whatever comes out of my house to greet me I will give it to you."

Now, understand the depth of this giving. Jephthah did not say, "I will go inside, find some nice trinket, and bring it out and offer it to you." No, he said, "Anything that comes out, God, belongs to you."

This was a desperate man. This was a man crying out to God, needing his prayer answered now. He didn't leaf through his prayer journal. He didn't get out the latest book on "Microwave Miracles Through Prayer." No, he reached deep down within himself. He knew that prayer mixed with giving immediately gets God's attention, because giving is an act of faith.

And so the Lord delivered Ammon into his hands. Jephthah did not have to wait months for an answer. More than 40,000 men were slaughtered that very day at the sword of Jephthah!

If we are ever to get the leaven out as we approach the end of the age, we must learn to mix our praying with sacrificial giving—giving that reflects the intensity of our heart to follow Christ.

In the midst of his imprisonment in the sewer systems of Rome, the Apostle Paul lifted up his voice and exclaimed, "God has highly exalted me and given me joint seating together with Christ in heavenly places."

If there's one thing Jephthah should teach us, it is that the devil is a coward who picks off the weak stragglers at the back of the pack. The Bible says, "Resist the devil, and he will flee from you" (James 4:7b). So stand strong, and he'll move on to easier pickings!

A SLEEPING GIANT

Let me illustrate where I believe the Church is and where it has the opportunity of going.

Many men have tried to conquer the world, but few have ever even come close to attaining that goal. Alexander the Great, at the age of 17, sat down on the portico steps of the great coliseum in Rome, put his head in his hands and wept. His generals rushed to his side and asked, "Why do you weep, Alexander?"

"Because," he cried, "there are no more worlds left to conquer."

Hitler tried. He committed heinous crimes, led six million Jews to the gas chambers and wrought havoc on the entire planet.

Another man came very close—Napoleon. It is said that he would gather his warlords together and spread out a map of the world. As they reviewed the map, suddenly his finger would rise in the air and plunge into the center of that map, always landing on a tiny red spot out in the middle of the ocean, a little place called England. As his finger landed on that red spot, his face would cringe and his voice would heighten until his warlords trembled. Napoleon would roar, "Were it not for that red spot, I could conquer the world!"

On a lonely hillside outside of Jerusalem a carpenter hung between heaven and earth. And there, the sun beat down into His open wounds until it felt as though the very flames of hell had embedded themselves in the flesh of the Son of God.

I believe that as Jesus hung there between heaven

CHAPTER 7 | THE CLEANSING SOLUTION

and earth, from the darkened regions of the demonic underworld, Satan raised his crooked finger and with a wicked glare, pointed toward Golgotha's hillside and screamed, "Were it not for that red spot, I could conquer the world!"

There's a red spot on the face of the earth today. That spot is a remnant of the New Testament Church, a remnant that is bold enough and brave enough to proclaim, "We're going to preach the old-fashioned Holy Ghost Gospel of Jesus Christ, whether the devil likes it or not!"

Thank God for preachers who will tell you that hell is real and eternity is long! Thank God for men who are not mere puppets, but are men who will get behind the sacred pulpit of God and begin to cry out as prophets of old!

I believe the John the Baptists of our generation are going to come out of the wilderness, crying loud and sparing not!

In 1815, Napoleon rolled out his map again before the Battle of Waterloo, and with his finger he traced the jagged edge of a great nation. He said, "Gentlemen, here lies a sleeping giant. If it ever recognizes its mineral wealth and ties it to its manpower, let the world bow its knee to it and tremble." He had outlined the nation of China. "A sleeping giant," he proclaimed, "Let it sleep. Let us not rouse it from its slumber."

In like manner, Satan is reviewing the map of the ages, and as he does, the corridors of hell ring with the words, "Let them wallow in the leaven of religiosity! Let them have their church socials, their committees, and all their plans and programs! Let them come to church and go home soothing their consciences! But if they ever wake up and understand the power of the blood and the authority of the name of Jesus, then we will be destroyed by this sleeping giant called The Church!"

PROCLAIM IT FROM THE ROOFTOPS!

The Bible does not say, "Whisper." The Bible does not say, "Be real nice, real soft, and real quiet, and try to be everyone's friend." The Bible does not say, "Try to fit in with the religious crowd; don't ruffle their feathers."

CHAPTER 7 | THE CLEANSING SOLUTION

No! The Bible says, "Cry aloud, do not hold back; lift up your voice like a trumpet, and show My people their transgression and the house of Jacob their sins" (Isaiah 58:1).

It is time for the Church to take a new step forward. God has a remnant on this planet of people who know His name—people who will stand up and declare, "It is time for the prophetic voice of God to ring out from the highest housetops! It's time to tell everyone, everywhere that there is only one way to heaven, and His name is Jesus!"

There is a group of us who want to keep and proclaim the Gospel. We are manning our battle stations.

We have heard the war cry of the great God Jehovah, and we are coming out of the cracks and crevices, out of buildings and byways, out of places hewn in rock and places dug in fear.

We have heard the trumpeting voice of God exclaim, "If I am for you, do not fear what men can do to you. For what can man do unto you if I am for you? No man can be against you, for greater is He that is in you than he that is in the world!"

There is only one reason why Communism fell from the former Soviet Union. That reason is idolatry. They raised mere mortals to the status of gods.

Look in God's Word. When idolatry is practiced in a nation, agricultural ruin follows. God withholds rain and sends plagues and hail and other pestilences of nature.

I was in Russia during the fall of the great Communist institutions. While preaching one of the first Gospel rallies in that country in more than 70 years, I raised my Bible and said, "This is a Bible! It tells of God's love and man's fall. Lenin came and went. Stalin came and went. Mussolini came and went. But God's Word is eternal!"

If we are going to get the leaven out of the Church, we are going to have to return to the basic tenets of the Bible. I know that in this philosophical age of theological mishmash, everyone has some new revelation. But I am not looking for new revelation. The greatest revelation from the Bible I have ever received is found in John 3:16:

"For God so loved the world that He gave His only begotten Son, that whoever believes in Him should not perish, but have eternal life."

You may say, "Well, I just do not believe in all that emotionalism."

Well, I'll bet if you received an unexpected $1,000 check, you'd believe in emotionalism real quick. So why not get emotional about Jesus? He owns the cattle on a thousand hills!

You may say, "Well now, Brother Rod, some people worship that way, some people get all excited. But not us, we're different, we're a little more genteel."

Fine. But I guarantee that if I put a paper clip in the hands of 100 people and let each of them stick his or her clip in a light socket, every one of them would have the same reaction. And it wouldn't be genteel. God's power is the same all over. We have been given power from on high!

It is time to proclaim that a resurrected Savior shed His blood for lost humanity. He is the only one who can get the leaven out of the Church today.

HE BROUGHT US OUT!

In the first five books of the Bible, God reminds the children of Israel 44 times, "I am the God who brought you out!"

The God we serve is still a saving Jesus. He is still a healing Jesus. He is still a delivering Jesus. And He can also take the leaven out.

In one moment, in one prayer, without the aid of any organization, He took an alcoholic of 35 years and cleaned him up, straightened him up and sobered him up, so that 15 years later he is still sitting on the edge of the third pew with his hands raised, never again touching one drop of alcohol. God took a $500 a day crack user, cleaned him up and put him in the church choir. He has led people out of homeless shelters and into salvation.

This is the God we serve. It is time someone started telling the truth about Jesus: He changes lives! He gets the leaven out!

WHERE IS THY STING?

So then, as the children share in flesh and

blood, He likewise took part in these, so that through death He might destroy him who has the power of death, that is, the devil, and deliver those who through fear of death were throughout their lives subject to bondage (Hebrews 2:14-15).

The last obstacle Jesus conquered was death. I once stood by the casket of a dear saint of God who died at the age of 88 years. She laid there in that casket, and when her family walked by, I told them, "If she could talk to us, she would say, 'Do not weep for me. I am in a country where there aren't any wheelchairs or funeral homes or morticians. There aren't any babies with swollen bellies. There are no street gangs nor drug wars.' She is now living in a city whose Builder and Maker is God, where there are no foes, no tears, no health problems, no growing old, no more death."

There is no foe bigger than death. The leaven of death is slow but certain. But through God and the power of His Son, who ascended on that heavenly throne, death has been grabbed by the nape of the neck and crushed!

Jesus declared, "I am Alpha. I am Omega. I was dead, but I am alive forevermore!" Jesus transcends the natural world. He transcends the polluting, corrosive effects of leaven.

With all our heart, mind, soul, and strength, let us revere Him. In Him, our hearts are free; there is no more fear of the past, the present, or the future. For what shall men do to us? If God is for us, who can be against us? He put demon hordes of hell under our feet. He made our bodies full of the healing power of Jesus. We have victory from the top of our heads to the soles of our feet. God made a way for us when there was no way. He slips His everlasting arms under us to keep us from falling. He bears us up on angels' wings. He has swallowed up death!

There are three kinds of death: physical death, spiritual death. and what the book of Revelation calls "the second death."

We can have all the leaven of the world, all the money a person could have, all the business prowess anyone could possess and all the respect of the world. But one day we will be staring physical death in the face and our eyes will close for the last time. One day we will lace our shoes for the last time, kiss our spouse goodbye for the last time, get in our car and drive to work for the very last time.

Many in this world throw up their hands and cry, "I don't know what is coming after that!"

Do you want to know what makes us Christians emotional? What makes us run? What makes us excited? We know what is coming after death!

You could take a gun, pull back the hammer, put your finger on the trigger and squeeze. That bullet could strike me with the force of death, instantly killing me. On that day, unless first Jesus comes for the rapture of the Church first, they are going to take my body, fold my hands over the top of my chest and lay me down in a casket. A few people may say, "Well, we will miss him."

If I could, I would wink at them. But do not weep for me! Do not feel sorrow for me! You might make my body fill a dirt hole in the ground, but you cannot kill me! I am alive forever! I am no longer subject to bondage through fear of physical death. Don't be dripping tears on this body, because my Jesus went to an old hill outside Jerusalem called Calvary, and He shed His life's blood for me!

Close by that scene we find the borrowed tomb of Joseph of Arimathaea. It is not significant because of Who is there. It's significant because of Who is not there.

On the third day a great angel said, "Mary, go and tell them that the Son of God is risen."

When Jesus rose from the dead He said, "I pried the keys of death and hell out of the hands of the Antichrist, and I rode out of the halls of the devil's perdition and right into heaven!"

If tomorrow death finds me missing, the Bible will tell you where I am. It declares that to be absent from the body is to be present with the Lord.

We can live without fear of death. We can wink at death's angel and say, "Transport me into the pavilions of glory prepared for me from the foundation of time. Thank you." Flip him a tip if you want.

CHAPTER 7 | THE CLEANSING SOLUTION

The Bible declares that the foundations of that heavenly city are not made of concrete and steel, but of the very finest precious jewels. But honestly, it wouldn't matter to me if the gates of heaven were made of wood or if they swung on leather hinges. It would not matter to me if there was knee-deep mud in the streets and the mansions were nothing more than cardboard shanties. Because when I look down the end of that muddy street, at the end of that heavenly boulevard, I will see the One who took my place.

When I deserved death, He cancelled my debt. When I deserved eternity in the bowels of hell, He sealed my pardon and marked my bill "Paid in Full." He tasted death, so that we, who through the fear of death are subject to bondage, could go free!

But we see Jesus, who was made a little lower than the angels to suffer death, crowned with glory and honor, so that He, by the grace of God, should experience death for everyone. So then, as the children share in flesh and blood, He likewise took part in these, so that through death He might destroy him who has the power of death, that is, the devil, and deliver those who through fear of death were throughout their lives subject to bondage. For surely He does not help the angels, but He helps the seed of Abraham (Hebrews 2:9, 14-16).

  I have an investment on the other side. I have a grandmamma, who was one of the greatest Christians I ever knew, waiting for me. I have a sister who spent years interceding for this ministry. I have a father who helped build every building on our church's property. And I have a mother who was the closest adviser I've ever had. I miss them all terribly. When I get to heaven, I will see them all again! And I will hug my grandmamma, my sister, my father, and my mother!

    In ancient Rome, a criminal who was found guilty of first-degree murder was forced to walk the streets with the body of the one he had murdered strapped to his own back. Finally, the decay of that body of death would infect the murderer's own body until he would die too.

Paul said, "That's the way it was with me. I was walking around with a body of death on me and I could not get it off. And I cried out, 'Who shall deliver me from this body of death? Who can take it off me?'"

"O wretched man that I am! Who will deliver me from the body of this death? For the law of the Spirit of life in Christ Jesus has set me free from the law of sin and death" (Romans 7:24; 8:2).

SPIRITUAL DEATH

We are in the last days. This is the grand finale. We are in the locker room for the pre-game briefing of the Super Bowl of the ages being played out on this planet between the forces of darkness and the forces of light.

Our Commander in Chief is standing, as a coach in the locker room before the big game, and He is saying: "I have some strategies for you. They are going to shoot the gap. Don't worry about it; we are going to double-team them. No, I'll tell you what we'll do. We'll triple-team them. The Father, the Son, and the Holy Ghost will block in front of us!"

But there is leaven, because we are carnal Christians. It is in our minds, our motives, and our ministries. We have to crucify it.

The Bible will deliver us from the fear and bondage of carnality and death. Only through the Word can we be free from the leaven Paul describes: backbiting, envy, strife, reveling, heresy, sedition, lust and murder. Paul could write that same message today to the church in Columbus, Miami, Orlando, Los Angeles, Dallas, Tallahassee, or New York. To be carnally minded is death.

THE SECOND DEATH

Then I saw a great white throne and Him who was seated on it. From His face the earth and the heavens fled away, and no place was found for them. And I saw the dead, small and great, standing before God. Books were opened. Then another book was opened, which is the Book of Life. The dead were judged according to their works as recorded in the books. The

CHAPTER 7 | THE CLEANSING SOLUTION

sea gave up the dead who were in it, and Death and Hades delivered up the dead who were in them. And they were judged, each one by his works. Then Death and Hades were cast into the lake of fire. This is the second death. Anyone whose name was not found written in the Book of Life was cast into the lake of fire (Revelation 20:11-15).

The third arena of death for which the cross of Christ secured our liberty is called the second death. God gave us absolute dominion over death. We, who through the fear of death were all our lifetime subject to bondage, have been freed—freed from physical death, freed from spiritual death, freed from carnality, and freed from the second death:

And I saw an angel coming down out of heaven, having the key to the bottomless pit and a great chain in his hand. He seized the dragon, that ancient serpent, who is the Devil and Satan, and bound him for a thousand years. He cast him into the bottomless pit, and shut him up, and set a seal on him, that he should deceive the nations no more, until the thousand years were ended. After that he must be set free for a little while. I saw thrones, and they sat on them, and the authority to judge was given to them. And I saw the souls of those who had been beheaded for their witness of Jesus and for the word of God. They had not worshipped the beast or his image, and had not received his mark on their foreheads or on their hands. They came to life and reigned with Christ for a thousand years

(Revelation 20:1-4).

During the time in the above Scripture, the rapture of the Church spoken of in 1 Thessalonians had transpired, and the Church of Jesus Christ had been around the throne of God for seven years, celebrating in the marriage supper of the Lamb. During that time the world had experienced seven years of the most horrendous tribulation ever to hit the earth. Jesus himself said, "For then will be great tribulation, such as has not happened since the beginning of the world until now, no, nor ever shall be" (Matthew 24:21).

The last day of the tribulation period becomes the first day of the millennial reign of Christ. God, will suddenly give the decree. Chariots that haven't ridden the wind since the days of Elijah will be pulled from their stalls. Jesus Christ Himself will arise from the marriage supper table. He'll mount a great white stallion, and the crack of His whip will billow out with the crash of a thousand cannons.

The Bible says He's coming back to this earth, and all His saints will be with Him. We are going to be riding with Him when He returns to this planet. Talk about victory over death! He's coming back! He's not coming wrapped in swaddling clothes and laid in a manager, and He won't be a longhaired, sandal-shoed, flowing-gowned person walking around the Sea of Galilee:

> *I saw heaven opened. And there was a white horse. He who sat on it is called Faithful and True, and in righteousness He judges and wages war. His eyes are like a flame of fire, and*

on His head are many crowns. He has a name written, that no one knows but He Himself. He is clothed with a robe dipped in blood. His name is called The Word of God. The armies in heaven, clothed in fine linen, white and clean, followed Him on white horses. Out of His mouth proceeds a sharp sword, with which He may strike the nations. "He shall rule them with an iron scepter." He treads the winepress of the fury and wrath of God the Almighty. On His robe and on His thigh He has a name written: KING OF KINGS AND LORD OF LORDS (Revelation 19:11-16).

Let the kings of the earth tremble, and the demon hordes quake in horror. The King of Glory shall come through! He has crushed the tormenting, demonic powers that have ruled this planet since Genesis 3. He has gathered His saints unto Himself from the four winds of the earth. They will be with Him when He comes back to defeat the Antichrist and his army in the Valley of Megiddo. Without lifting His sword, He'll look across that valley and speak one word. The Bible says in Zechariah 14:12,

> *And this will be the pestilence with which the LORD will strike all the peoples who go to battle against Jerusalem: Their flesh will rot as they stand on their feet, their eyes will rot in their sockets, and their tongues will rot in their mouths.*

He is coming down through the Kidron Valley, through the eastern gate to Temple Mount, where He will rule and reign for 1,000 years of peace. And then, at the end of that time, will come the judgment, and the second death.

If you choose to go to hell, you will be an intruder upon Satan and his hordes for all eternity. hell was not made for humans!

So many people are confused about the last book of the Bible, but there is no reason to be confused. In fact, if there was any generation in the history of the world that should understand the book of Revelation, it is this one. God wrote it for us. We are watching the prophecy being fulfilled every day. Thank God for it.

Leavened or Unleavened? The choice we have today is God or the devil, heaven or hell, life or death, blessing or cursing, leavened or unleavened.

If we choose Christ, then hell, death, cursing and leaven have no power on us. But if we reject Him, we will stand at the Great White Throne of Judgment and stare at a gaping, unbearable blankness in the Book of Life, and we will say in our heart, "There it is. That's the place where my name could have been, where Jesus Christ the Son of God stood poised and ready to enter my name. But I said, 'No.'"

In this end time hour of spiritual history, it is time to shun the shallow flatlands of spiritual mediocrity and go all the way with Jesus.

Will you examine your heart? If it is not on fire for God, if you are not excited about the things of God, if you do not feel the life and power of God in every part and portion of your being, then pray: "Dear God, deliver me from the leaven of death and make me eternally alive!" And you can be certain that He will!

LET YOUR HEART HOLD HOPE!

He gave some to be apostles, prophets, evangelists, pastors, and teachers, for the equipping of the saints, for the work of service, and for the building up of the body of Christ, until we all come into the unity of the faith and of the knowledge of the Son of God, into a complete man, to the measure of the stature of the fullness of Christ (Ephesians 4:11-13).

Even in Biblical times, there came a lull in the prophetic voices of the nation of Israel. The children of Israel could only find Dr. Sounding Brass and Dr. Fog Horn, trying to dissuade them from the realities of the Word of God. And so it seems to be happening today.

The thundering voices of the prophets seem to be waning. Are we losing sight of old-fashioned, Holy Ghost-inspired preaching? Where are the Billy Sundays, the Lakes, Finneys, and Moodys of the new millennium?

The Church is growing out of balance in the ministry gifts. There have been an abundance of teachers in the ministry. But we do not have enough of the rest of the five-fold ministry gifts in the body of Christ. Teachers are vitally important, but God intended for all of the ministry gifts to be manifested in His New Testament Church, not just the ministry of teachers. Is it just my imagination, or do we have few people willing to reach one hand into glory and the other into the gutter to rescue depraved, dying, desperate humanity from the abyss of hell?

But my heart holds hope today: not all of the unflinching men of God have vanished from the earth! They are being revived and refueled! The Church is waking up! We are more determined! We are bolder! We are holding up the blood-stained banner of the cross of Christ and trampling the devil under our feet, pursuing, overtaking and recovering all that Satan thinks he took from us!

My heart holds hope that the Church is ready to cleanse and purify itself of all leaven.

BE YE UNLEAVENED!

The way to a life free of leaven is through the

simple, plain, unadulterated Gospel.

God created man, but man committed sin and high treason against God and fell in the Garden of Eden. At that moment, God began to build a bridge, a bridge that would bring men and women back to a place of fellowship with Him.

Oh, that we would all cross the Gospel bridge, restored and purified of leaven, and cry out to God: "Lord, let your holy anointing rest upon us like a mantle. Let the anointing that destroys every yoke come upon us. Let us wear it like a garment. Let your supernatural power flow from our bellies. Let your healing power shoot from our hands like lightning from a dark-throated thunderstorm."

May we raise up a remnant Church that will be a light to the entire world. May every stronghold of Satan tremble as we get up each morning. May those frozen by the icy grip of religious tradition begin to thaw under Your prophetic voice."

Let's stop trying to get across the Bridge through religiosity. Let's stop trying to go through life full of the leaven of Pharisees, the Sadducees, Galatians, Herodians and Corinthians.

Judgment stares each of us in the face. The road of life inevitably ends up at the crossroads of the cross. No one bypasses the cross.

God cannot bless us beyond our last act of disobedience, beyond our last taste of leavened bread. Do you attend a Bible-teaching, Holy Spirit-filled, Jesus-loving church? Join!

Do you help God's children? Serve!

Do you study the Word of God daily? Read!

Do you talk with the Lord every day? Pray!

Do you tithe? Start!

So many Christians today are like the prodigal son. They want the Father's possessions, but they do not want the Father's presence. They want what He has, but they do not want Him.

We have a marvelous road map called the Bible. All we need to do is read it, and follow it. We don't need the evening news. Just read the Bible, and you will know the news before it happens.

I pray the religious dead will find life in Christ. But if they never do, they still cannot stop revival. They cannot stop the outpouring of the Holy Ghost. They cannot stop the signs and wonders that are destined for this generation. They cannot stop us from getting all the leaven out of our lives once and for all. The greatest revival we have ever seen, heard, or read is about to begin.

It is time for us to wake up and walk in the power and glory of God!

NOTES

Chapter 1
How Spiritual Deterioration Contaminates the Unsuspecting Church

1. Giankaris, C.J., *Plutarch*. New York, New York: Twayn Publishers, Inc., 1970.

2. Foxe, John, "Wendelmuta, A Widow." <u>Foxe's Book of Martyrs</u>, London: Adam & Company, 14 Ivy Lane, Paternoster Row, and Newcastle-Uper-Tyne, n.d., 159-160.

3. Ibid.

4. Ravenhill, Leonard, <u>Revival God's Way</u>. Minneapolis, Minnesota: Bethany House Publishers, 1986, 50

Chapter 3
The Leaven of the Sadducees

1. "The Generation That Forgot God: The Baby Boom Goes Back to Church and Church Will Never Be the Same." Time. 5 April 1993, 44-49.

2. Stanphill, Ira F. "Mansion Over the Hilltop." Cited from *Melodies of Praise*, Springfield, Missouri: Gospel Publishing House, 1957, 45.

ROD PARSLEY is the author of more than seventy books, and host of the daily television broadcast *Breakthrough*, viewed by millions worldwide. He is the founder of various ministries, including Valor Christian College, Bridge of Hope missions, and City Harvest Network. The role closest to his heart is that of senior pastor and founder of World Harvest Church in Columbus, Ohio, where he resides with his wife, Joni, and their two adult children.

Learn more about Rod Parsley at **www.rodparsley.com**

Connect on Social Media: @RodParsley @RealRodParsley

SEEK TRUTH IN A GENERATION GIVEN TO EXTREMES

It's true that Christians are freed from the rule of the law. Yet it is also true that the law is a revelation of God's will. How can we lead godly lives and also avoid turning moral absolutes into a legalistic system for salvation?

In *Grace*, Rod Parsley uncovers the tension surrounding conversations about grace so that you can:

- Gain biblical foundation of God's true intention for law and grace
- Live more powerfully by avoiding destructive extremes
- Adopt principles for Christian living that come from Scripture and the work of the Holy Spirit in your heart
- Understand moments in church history when these issues threatened to destroy faith, formed new doctrines and denomonations .... *and more!*

GRACE

UNCOVERED.
UNFILTERED.
UNDESERVED.

ROD PARSLEY

TO ORDER VISIT **RODPARSLEY.COM/GRACE**

BE MADE WHOLE

This double-volume set is a reproduction of the Scripture book God used to sustain Pastor Rod Parsley through his battle with cancer!

Request yours today! Call **855.641.8859**
or go to **www.RodParsley.com/HealingSet**